PRISONER VOICES FROM DEATH ROW

This book is dedicated to all prisoners currently on death row and who were on death row in India

This book is also a tribute to two of my beloved research participants whom I interviewed in Nagpur Central Prison – Yakub Abdul Razak Memon, who was executed and Ajith Singh Gujral who died of natural causes.

Prisoner Voices from Death Row

Indian Experiences

REENA MARY GEORGE

Routledge
Taylor & Francis Group
LONDON AND NEW YORK

First published 2015 by Ashgate Publishing

2 Park Square, Milton Park, Abingdon, Oxfordshire OX14 4RN
52 Vanderbilt Avenue, New York, NY 10017

Routledge is an imprint of the Taylor & Francis Group, an informa business

First issued in paperback 2020

British Library Cataloguing in Publication Data
A catalogue record for this book is available from the British Library.

The Library of Congress has cataloged the printed edition as follows:
George, Reena Mary.
Prisoner voices from death row : Indian experiences / by Reena Mary George.
pages cm
Includes bibliographical references and index.
ISBN 978-1-4724-6172-8 (hardback)
1. Death row inmates—India. 2. Capital punishment—India.
3. Criminal justice, Administration of—India. I. Title.
HV8699.I4G46 2015
364.66092'254–dc23

2015016067

ISBN: 978-1-4724-6172-8 (hbk)
ISBN: 978-0-367-59777-1 (pbk)

Contents

List of Tables

Foreword

Manfred Nowak

In my capacity as UN Special Rapporteur on Torture between 2004 and 2010 I visited many prisons in all regions of the world and spoke in private to innumerable detainees. My main aim was to investigate practices of torture. But when I asked prisoners whether they had been subjected to torture, I often received an answer on the following lines: 'Of course, I have been tortured by the police after having been arrested. It was terrible, but it stopped as soon as I had confessed to the crime they accused me of. The suffering I have since then been enduring for years in these overcrowded and dirty cells, without light, fresh air, sufficient food or health care, where we are held in conditions worse than animals, is, however, a hundred times worse than the physical pain during two nights of police torture'. In fact, the conditions of detention in the 21st century are so terrible that I spoke in my final report about a 'global prison crisis' and demanded that the United Nations draft and adopt an international treaty on the rights of detainees. Prison walls serve a double purpose: They lock prisoners in and society out. In fact, most people are happy that they do not know what life behind prison walls actually looks like. We lack empathy for those behind prison walls. People who are locked away by the State must have committed terrible crimes and, therefore, do not deserve our empathy. But reality tells a different story. To become a prisoner usually is the 'privilege of the poor'. Prisons, and the administration of 'justice' in more general terms, figure among the most corrupt sectors of society in many countries in all world regions. If a crime is committed, considerable pressure is put on the police by judges, prosecutors, politicians, the media and society at large to 'solve' this crime by finding the perpetrators and bringing them to justice. In most countries, the police are not well-educated, well-paid and lack more sophisticated means of evidence taking, such as DNA analysis. Police officers simply arrest people who look suspicious, such as homeless and jobless people, persons with a criminal background, members of minorities and other scapegoats. If they do not confess to the crime, they are subjected to torture in order to extract such a confession. Then these torture survivors disappear behind prison walls, often for years in pre-trial detention, before they are finally convicted by a court on the basis of their 'confession' signed during police interrogation. If you have enough money, you are usually not arrested in the first place. Should you, however, be arrested, you may find a police officer, prosecutor, judge, prison guard or politician whom you can bribe to go free. Sometimes, such bribes are called 'bail'.

Conditions on death row are the worst. In Mongolia, I discovered that persons condemned to capital punishment had to spend the last months of their lives, handcuffed and shackled, in dark solitary confinement cells without any contacts to the outer world. They were only allowed to see one family member before they were executed. I was shocked, demanded abolition and am grateful that the Government in the meantime has abolished this cruel punishment. In China, I also interviewed various death row prisoners, who were handcuffed and shackled, but at least not kept in solitary confinement. While death row prisoners were held in overcrowded and dirty cells in Nigeria, their condition seemed to be less inhuman than in countries like Jamaica, where they are kept in solitary confinement cells in maximum security prison wings. In Jordan, I talked to an Iraqi woman in solitary confinement, who was executed soon after my visit. Whenever I recently hear that another drug offender is going to be executed in Indonesia, I look into my files to see whether I had interviewed him almost 10 years ago on a remote prison island south of Java. Death row prisoners will always remain in my memory. I still see the faces of these drug offenders from various countries when we asked them whether they had lodged a complaint against their inhuman conditions of detention: 'To whom shall we complain? To the animals?' Even in Europe, which is proud to be the first death penalty free zone in the world, I have still visited death row prisoners in the Russian-controlled territories of Abkhazia (Georgia) and Transnistria (Moldova). When I asked the guards in an old, humid and dirty prison in Abkhazia to open the door of a death row cell in the basement, two strong men had to work on this rusty door for more than ten minutes. This door had certainly not been opened for more than a year, and the man I found behind this door seemed to be already in a different world filled with religious symbols. In Transnistria, we needed to find three different guards with different keys to open the cell of a death row prisoner whom I had to interview with handcuffs locked behind his back. But he was so handy and so much used to a life with handcuffs that he could offer me a cigarette and even light his cigarette himself. To speak with death row prisoners is a strong emotional experience. Prison guards and politicians make you believe that these people are the 'worst of the worst', the most dangerous individuals on earth. But when I managed, usually against the strong resistance of prison guards who cared so much about my personal safety, to speak with them in private, they were not different from other prisoners: human beings whose lives had been destroyed by a long chain of negative, and usually highly painful events.

Reena Mary George is a strong and brave woman with empathy for the poor, the underprivileged and the excluded. When we started our interdisciplinary PhD School 'Empowerment of the Poor' in 2009 at Vienna University, we had to select the 12 best candidates out of a total of 335 applicants from all over the world. We selected Reena after a long skype interview in which she had convinced us about her project aimed at giving death row prisoners in her native India a voice. When we asked her how she would succeed to convince the Indian authorities to provide her access to death row prisoners, she answered with a smiling face: 'I will convince them'. And she did. Out of 186 prisoners on death row in 2011, she managed to interview not less than 111 in 16 prisons from six federal States of India! This alone is already a remarkable achievement for a young female researcher working in such a heavily male-dominated micro-cosmos. In addition to gaining access to the opaque prison world, she also succeeded in getting the informed consent of her interview partners and, thereby, providing the 'voiceless' with a public voice. Finally, her interdisciplinary research work led to a number of important findings, which strongly coincide with my own experience and research work. In particular, she concludes that 'social exclusion, marginalisation and poverty are antecedents to death penalty', and that the 'death penalty is a phenomenon constructed by the state machinery'. But the main theme of her study was to uphold the dignity of death row prisoners by simply listening to their stories and making their voices heard. That is why it is so important that her study will now be published by Ashgate Publishing.

I sincerely hope that this book will contribute to the abolition of capital punishment in India and worldwide. The death penalty as the ultimate form of a cruel and inhuman punishment is a remnant of medieval 'justice' and has no longer any place in the modern and enlightened world of the 21st century! Finally, I wish Reena much success in her professional life which will always aim at the empowerment of the poor.

Vienna, May 2015

Preface

'I want to be brave; I want to be courageous. I do not want to be afraid to walk among prisoners'. I wanted to be like Elizabeth Fry, the nineteenth century prison reformer who was not afraid of anything. I wanted to be brave like her. This was my only motivation for working in prison. I began working with women prisoners and the children of prisoners in two prisons as a student social worker at the age of 22. This was in Mumbai through an organisation that worked for the rehabilitation of prisoners. I was certainly there because of the 'exoticism' of the prison and the 'other'. However, soon I realised there was nothing exotic about it. It was the reality of their lives – women prisoners being separated from their children, partners leaving them, their children on the streets begging; being molested. It wasn't exotic anymore.

I could not cope with women convicted of killing their own babies or murdering their husbands because of an affair. I found it very cruel. At the same time, working with recidivist women prisoners exposed me to a few more realities of life – poverty, helplessness and other social circumstances that drive women to engage in crimes. For me it was shocking to hear about crimes of passion. I was further shocked to hear that children of women prisoners lived on the street, I was aghast to find a five year old boy locked in a house and who ate wheat grains to survive. We eventually placed him in a children's home. Even after ten years of working in this area, I am still shocked to hear about the experiences of prisoners. I once talked to a mentally disturbed woman prisoner alone and my supervisor told me that I was risking my life by putting myself in that situation.

These experiences occurred in 2004 when Dhanojoy Chatterjee was hanged to death. My teacher Professor Dr Vandana Chakrabarti initiated a debate in our class over the issue of the death penalty. I realised that there is no shade of grey with the death penalty. Either you are for it or against it. I was the latter in the debate. Over the years, I continued my research with women prisoners and their children. During this period I read a lot on torture in custody. This was also precisely the time when the Abu Ghraib incident came to light. Around this time, I read a statement by Manfred Nowak which said that the United States has a clear obligation to prosecute Bush and Rumsfeld. I was impressed that someone spoke the truth. My thought process shifted to the death penalty as a form of torture. This was 2008.

I was doing a post-graduate diploma in human rights and chose the death penalty as my topic for research. I interviewed 13 prisoners who were on death row in Maharashtra under the guidance of retired Bombay High Court Judge, Hosbet Suresh. This was the first small-scale study on the human rights perspective of the death penalty conducted in Maharashtra. This was also the time where I worked in an organisation where one of my tasks was to conduct a fact-finding mission in cases of custodial death and it wasn't unusual to conduct fact findings of people dying in custody. I completed the study and at the end of 2009, I was happy to see a doctoral programme for which Manfred was the Speaker. I was selected in 2010 and was one of the 12 Research Fellows at the Initiative College 'Empowerment through Human Rights' at the University of Vienna. I left my home town – Mumbai- to come to Vienna in March 2010. I started my doctorate within an interdisciplinary group. My fellows researched other topics pertaining to human rights such as the psychological impact of torture on its victims, the problems of Romas, issues of asylum-seekers, African scholarship on human rights and development, intellectual disability, children's rights and drug use, business and human rights, trafficking in human beings and women's property rights. I found that each of them was just as crazy as me and I learned a great deal from them.

Within four months of my coming to Vienna, I started sending letters seeking permission from the Indian authorities to conduct a study with prisoners on death row. Eventually by the end of 2010, I started receiving permission from states to conduct the study. I started to prepare for my field work which began in February 2011. For five months I travelled the length and breadth of India. In August 2011, I came back to Vienna. I had with me notes on spine-chilling experiences narrated by prisoners. I had their voices captured and I wanted to bring it out. At the 2004 Sydney Peace Prize lecture Arundhati Roy, an author and an ardent activist said, 'There's really no such thing as the "voiceless". There are only the deliberately silenced or the preferably unheard'. Voices of prisoners whom we hardly know were not to be deliberately silenced or preferably unheard. Most people think of prisoners as people who are dangerous and incapable of reform, however there is a lot of pain and humiliation that prisoners go through and that needs to be highlighted. Hence, the book begins with the aims of the study-the highs and lows of the debate on death penalty with dignity as the main theme. Justice Hosbet Suresh, retired Bombay High Court Judge and my mentor says, '*Though I was empowered to give the death sentence, I was not qualified to impose the same. How could I be an instrument of the State to take away somebody's life, when I do not know the person at all, excepting the crime that s/he has been charged with?*' It was important not to silence or 'unhear' the stories. This led to my articulation of the methods and ethical concerns that the study was guided by. Furthermore, hearing the voices of prisoners, my heart skipped a beat. It still skips a beat when I think of the painful accounts and the tears that I saw. It is difficult for me digest when news reports says that the prisoner shows no remorse. When one spends enough time with them, one sees that they indeed feel terrible about what happened and regret it each moment or at least when they sleep at night.

Scheper-Hughes[1] deliberates that as researchers, we are in the field to observe, to document, to understand and later to write about the lives and the pain (of research participants) as fully, as truthfully and as sensitively as we can. Hence, she asks, 'What exempts us from the human responsibility to take an ethical and even a political stand on events as we are privileged to witness them?'. For instance when Manfred (Nowak) served as the United Nations Special Rapporteur on Torture, he gave an interview in a German Television programme. He made a statement that George W. Bush and Donald Rumsfeld should be prosecuted as they had violated human rights norms when speaking about prison torture. This was Manfred's human responsibility to take an ethical and even a political stand when he enquired about torture.

Scheper-Hughes wrote that what drew her to the people and places was not the exoticism and their 'otherness' but the pursuit of those small spaces of convergence, recognition and empathy that they share and that they are not so radically 'other' to each other. Even though it was the exoticism that drew me to research this topic, in the end it was about the spaces of convergence and recognition that I shared with the prisoners on death row. I also take a political stand on what I witnessed; I am against the death penalty for all sorts of crimes.

There are various reasons to oppose the death penalty – innocent people held guilty, deterrence, lack of capability for reform and so on and so forth. My reason for this stand is – The State cannot kill a person whom it is supposed to protect. Like Scheper-Hughes, I have taken sides and made judgments, even though taking sides or making judgments flies in the face of the 'non-engagement' principles of research. Scheper-Hughes goes a step further where she suggests that we can make ourselves available not just as friends or as 'patrons' in the old colonialist sense but as *comrade(s)*; with all the demands and responsibilities that this word implies; to the people who are the subjects of our writings, whose lives and miseries provide us with a livelihood. She suggests that we be a *companheira*. My way of being a *companheira* is by foregrounding and bringing out the generally stifled voices which prisoners and their families shared with me.

1 Scheper-Hughes, Nancy. 'The primacy of the ethical: propositions for a militant anthropology'. *Current Anthropology* 36, no. 3 (1995): 409–40.

Acknowledgements

I thank God for helping me to embark this journey and bring it to fruition. I thank my research participants – the prisoners on death row, who trusted me and shared their lives with me. I looked for convergences between their lives and mine and I tried to capture their voice. But in the end, I think I also found my voice. Thank you all for being open and allowing me to participate in your lives. I thank all the prison officials and Home Affairs Department of the State of Assam, Karnataka, Kerala, Maharashtra, Punjab and Tamil Nadu. I would also like to place on record my thanks to the Kurzfristige wissenschaftliche Arbeiten im Ausland (KWA) (Short term travel grant) that I received from the University of Vienna for my field work. Also I would like to thank the Research Platform on Human Rights and University of Vienna for the financial assistance in the form of employment and reimbursements.

In addition to this, I would like to thank the following people for supporting me during this journey: Manfred Nowak, Christoph Reinprecht, Justice Hosbet Suresh, Claire Jarvis, Sarah Charters, Peter Wagner, Rebecca Gonsalves, Vijay Hiremath, Vandana Chakrabarti, Asha Patil, Stefano Polacco, Miri Sharon, Michal Ružička, Andrea Fritsche, Simon Flacks, Julia Planitzer, Andreas Kranebitter, Manash Gogoi, John Robinson, Karthik SN, Renuka Srivastava, Aji Eapen, Judith Shaila Lobo, N.K. Prabhakaran, George Thomas, Aileen Hackl, Hyacinth Österlin, Patrick Curran, Sandra Weber, Ella Haiss, Rupp Hutter, Rudi Kocher, Sophia Kurien, Simon Baur, Julian Ricker, Caroline Weerkamp, Jurian Weerkamp, Rene Murschenhofer, Jacob Thomas (Sunny Achen), Hanka Krenčeyová, Ivan Krenčey, Marlies Fritsche, Milan Vesley, Sylvia Bartels, Miša Krenčeyová, Jitha Nair, P.J. George, Rachel George, Jilesh Cherian, Renu Merin George and Rashmi Lee George.

A special acknowledgement goes to my sister Rashmi Lee George who has stood by me from the beginning and supported my every decision. Thank you RC, without you this would not have been possible.

Chapter 1
Intonation of the Study

Introduction and Background of the Problem

I came across a quote in the context of the death penalty often attributed to Mahatma Gandhi, regarded as the Father of the Indian Nation. He said 'an eye for an eye makes the whole world blind' and I found it ironic that Mahatma Gandhi's assassins were also hanged to death. During a debate on the death penalty in my social work class when Dhanojoy Chatterjee was executed, I felt it was preposterous that the State could take anybody's life. This was also deeply linked to my thoughts concerning, 'What does the person to be hanged go through'? 'How is the person's dignity safeguarded'? The concept of 'dignity' is an omnipresent component of debates about the death penalty. It is a 'vague but powerful idea'[1] that influences and defines the direction of the death penalty dialogue, in no small part because its vagueness and power enable it to be invoked in support of myriad different views. The most commonly accepted understanding of dignity is the one that depicts it as an inalienable element of humanity, without which a person ceases to have any worth – physical, psychological, or moral. A person is nothing without his/her dignity.[2]

From time to time there are reports in the media concerning prisoners on death row in India but mostly these reports are narratives by prison officials, hence we know a great deal about these 'criminals' before they are awarded the death sentence.[3] We know their 'stories' from the media or 'facts of the crime' from court documents. However we do not know the person behind these 'stories' or 'facts' of crime. The issue of the death penalty was lying low in India

1 Dworkin, Ronald. *Taking Rights Seriously*. Harvard University Press, 1978; cited in Knowles, Helen J. 'A dialogue on death penalty dignity'. *Criminology and Criminal Justice* 11, no. 2 (2011): 115–28.

2 Beyleveld, Deryck and Roger Brownsword. *Human Dignity in Bioethics and Biolaw*. Oxford: Oxford University Press, 2001; Whitman, James Q. 'The two western cultures of privacy: Dignity versus liberty'. *Yale Law Journal* 113 (2003): 1151–221.

3 Sarang, Dastane et al. 'Ajmal Kasab loses composure at gallows, seeks forgiveness', *The Times of India* 22 November 2012. See http://articles.timesofindia.indiatimes.com/2012-11-22/mumbai/35301740_1_ajmal-kasab-yerwada-jail-mumbai-s-arthur-road (last accessed 23 November 2013).

after the execution of Dhanojoy Chatterjee[4] also known as Dhana in 2004. Dhana was convicted and executed for the rape and murder of an 18-year-old woman; however, Dhana maintained until his death that he was innocent. There were many newspaper reports which indicated the age of the victim as a 13–14-year-old schoolgirl whereas the judgment states the victim was an 18 year old woman. In the recent past, the death penalty has generated immense public debate. At the end of May 2011, the ex-President Pratibha Patil rejected the mercy petitions of Professor Devinder Pal Singh Bhullar[5] and Mahendra Nath Das.[6] A mercy petition is sent to the Governor or the President seeking pardon or mercy after all the appeals have exhausted.

Prof. Bhullar was sentenced to death in 2001 for the plotting terrorist attacks that killed nine people in Delhi in 1993, while Das has been on death row since 1997 for committing a murder in Guwahati, Assam, in 1996. A further three mercy petitions of Murugan, Santhan and Arivu alias Perarivalan of the Rajiv Gandhi assassination were rejected by the President in August 2011.[7] They were sentenced to death in January 1998 by a Special Anti-Terrorist Court and had their sentences confirmed by the Supreme Court of India in May 1999. The common factor for all of the above cases was that their mercy petition was with the President for a long period of time. Even though the President rejected the mercy petitions for the above prisoners, executions for these prisoners were suspended by the courts. This was to allow consideration of separate legal challenges on the delay in the decision of the mercy petitions and the constitutionality of their prolonged stay on death row.

With the rejection of mercy petitions, the debate on the death penalty started gaining momentum. The next wave of public opinion on the death penalty accelerated after the 'secret' execution of Ajmal Kasab on 21 November 2012. The news of Ajmal Kasab's execution appeared in media broadcasts (print and electronic) only after his death. The State kept his execution hidden. Ajmal was the lone surviving 'gun-man' of the Mumbai Terror Attacks in 2008. After Ajmal's execution, people celebrated his execution as one would celebrate festivals in India – with drum beats, crackers and colours. At the same time there was a group of individuals criticising the barbaric and secretive execution of Ajmal. Added to the debate was the 'secret' execution of Afzal Guru on 9th February 2013. His family was not informed about his execution in time, hence they did not have an opportunity to meet him for the last time; nor did he have a chance to tell

4 Dhananjoy Chatterjee Alias Dhana v State Of West Bengal, 2004 All MR (Cri) 2185 (SC); AIR 2004 SC 3435: 2004 Cr LJ 2827:2004 AIR SCW 3051.

5 State of Punjab v Devinder Pal Singh Bhullar & Ors. etc., AIR 2012 SC 364.

6 Mahendra Nath Das v The Union of India and Others Writ Petition (Crl) No. 35/2011.

7 Union Of India v Sriharan @, Murugan & Ors Writ Petition (Crl) No. 48 OF 2014.

them goodbye. His body was not returned to the family for last rites and burial, in violation of international standards. Afzal was convicted for the attack on the Indian Parliament in 2001.[8] Serious concerns about the fairness of Afzal Guru's trial – including the fact that he did not receive legal representation of his choice or a lawyer with adequate experience at the trial stage – were not addressed. Afzal Guru was also denied the opportunity to seek a judicial review of the decision to reject his mercy petition.[9] Finally, the gang-rape and eventual death of '*Nirbhaya*' (Delhi rape and murder victim) added impetus to the public opinion on the death penalty where it was suggested to undertake chemical castration for rapists before their execution.[10] The only thing that people demanded when these rapes occurred was death penalty. There is hardly any discussion on the rape culture that exists in India. People who demanded justice for Nirbhaya forgot Suzette Jordan[11] or the journalist[12] who worked with Tehelka and was allegedly raped by Tarun Tejpal. People also forget to demand justice for the mother and daughter in a Dalit family in Khairlanji, Maharashtra in 2006. Dalit is a designation for a group of people traditionally regarded as untouchable in the Indian caste system. The mother and the daughter were stripped, paraded naked, beaten black and blue with bicycle chains, axes and bullock cart pokers in public. They were publicly gang raped until they died. Some raped them even after that and finally, sticks and rods were shoved into their genitals. The two sons of the same Dalit family were beaten up, their genitals mutilated, faces disfigured and their bodies tossed in the air, before they lay dead on the ground.[13] No one seems

8 Roy, Arundhati. 'A perfect day for democracy', *The Hindu*, 10 February 2013. See http://www.thehindu.com/opinion/lead/a-perfect-day-for-democracy/article4397705.ece?homepage=true (last accessed 25 March 2015).

9 Amnesty International Report. 'Death sentences and executions 2011', London. Index number: ACT 50/001/2012. See https://www.amnesty.org/en/documents/ACT50/001/2012/en/ (last accessed 25 March 2015).

10 Press Trust of India. 'Congress draft anti-rape law proposes chemical castration', *India Today* 30 December 2012. See http://indiatoday.intoday.in/story/congress-draft-anti-rape-law-proposes-chemical-castration/1/240107.html (last accessed 4 January 2015).

11 Singh, Shiv Sahay. 'Park Street rape survivor Suzette Jordan dies', *The Hindu*, 14 March 2015. See http://www.thehindu.com/news/national/park-street-rape-victim-dies/article6989762.ece (last accessed 17 March 2015).

12 Agency: IANS. 'Tehelka founder and editor-in-chief Tarun Tejpal charged with rape, says he will aid probe', *DNA* 22 November 2013. See http://www.dnaindia.com/india/report-tehelka-founder-and-editor-in-chief-tarun-tejpal-charged-with-rape-says-he-will-aid-probe-1923326 (last accessed 17 March 2015).

13 Vij, Shivam. 'Dalits, like flies to feudal lords', *Tehelka* 4 November 2006. See http://archive.tehelka.com/story_main22.asp?filename=Ne111106Dalits_like.asp (last accessed 23 March 2013).

to ask for the death penalty here, nobody's conscience seem to be disturbed. Similarly, no one has any pangs of conscience when it came to Soni Sori. Soni was in police custody where Ankit Garg was the Police Superintendent in Chhattisgarh. Newspaper reports said that he verbally abused Soni and directed police personnel to torture her. She alleged that Garg watched as junior police personnel stripped her naked, administered electric shocks and assaulted her. According to her lawyers, a medical examination found two stones in Soni's genital tract and another in her rectum. No action was taken against the police officer – Ankit Garg was awarded the Police Medal for Gallantry in 2012 for his raid on Maoist supporters.[14]

The death penalty has produced endless discourse not only in the context of prisons, prisoners and punishment but also in the legal arena – about the validity of death penalty: right to life, torture, and so on and so forth. The death penalty is embodied in Indian law. However, there is very little known about the people who are on death row except for media reports on them. This book sheds light on the experiences and perception of prisoners on death row in India and focuses on the narratives by prisoners on death row, especially the trajectory of their lives after they are arrested. This book also seeks to illuminate the situation of death row prisoners and the culture of the death penalty through their voices. It contains four chapters based on empirical research. In India the death penalty is hardly discussed in public discourse and majority of people believe in an 'eye for an eye and a tooth for a tooth' philosophy. This book describes how death row prisoners undergo the pains of imprisonment in a 'total', 'complete' and 'austere' institution; entangled in the web of state machinery and wedged in the predicament of death and dignity. Central to the study is the view that the prisoner is unknown to the world except for the crime that s/he is alleged to have committed. Justice Suresh, a retired Bombay High Court judge says that, *'Though I was empowered to give the death sentence, I was not qualified to impose the same. How could I be an instrument of the State to take away somebody's life, when I do not know the wo/man, at all, excepting the crime that s/he has been charged with'?*[15] In order to explore the way the prisoners on death row experience and perceive their lives and make meaning of that world, this book is underpinned by theories of phenomenology and symbolic interactionism.

---

14 Sethi, Aman. 'Activists shocked at gallantry award for Chhattisgarh cop', *The Hindu* 14 February 2012. See http://www.thehindu.com/news/national/article2834675.ece (last accessed 23 March 2015).

15 Ghormode, Vijay. *Death Sentence: A Struggle for Abolition*. Pune: Hind Law Publications, 2008.

Specific Objectives and Clarification of Terms

The main objective of the study was to enquire if the dignity of the prisoners was upheld while confronting the criminal justice system and while surviving on death row. Along with these the more specific objectives were, firstly, to understand the profiles of prisoners on death row; secondly to understand the stages prisoners experienced before being sentenced to death and thirdly to explore how prisoners perceived and experienced their conditions on death row. There are various terms used in the study which need clarification for a consistent understanding of the topic. The following are a list of terms used throughout the study.

Death Penalty/Capital Punishment

Death penalty is the ultimate punishment imposed for murder or other capital offenses.[16] In India, capital punishment is embodied in the Indian Penal Code, 1860 and the Criminal Procedure Code, 1973 and one is executed by hanging.[17] The term death penalty and capital punishment are used interchangeably in this book.

Death Row Phenomenon/Syndrome

The 'death row phenomenon' or 'death row syndrome' is a combination of circumstances found on death row that produces severe mental trauma and physical deterioration in prisoners under those sentences. This phenomenon or syndrome is a result of the harsh conditions experienced on death row, the length of time that they have experienced and the anxiety of awaiting one's own execution.[18] Other associated factors that contribute to the mental trauma include a cramped environment of deprivation, arbitrary rules, harassment and isolation from others.[19]

---

16 Gifis, Steven H. *Barron's Law Dictionary*. Hauppauge, NY: Barron's Educational Series, Inc., 2010.

17 Areti, Krishna Kumari. '*Capital Punishment and Statutory Frame Work in India*'. See http://works.bepress.com/krishnaareti/9 (2007) (last accessed 31 July 2015).

18 Hudson, Patrick. 'Does the death row phenomenon violate a prisoner's human rights under international law?'. *European Journal of International Law* 11, no. 4 (2000): 833–56.

19 Cunningham, Mark D. and Mark P. Vigen. 'Death row inmate characteristics, adjustment and confinement: A critical review of the literature'. *Behavioural Sciences & the Law* 20, no. 1–2 (2002): 191–210.

Death Row

Death row is the cell or block of cells in which prisoners condemned to death are held while awaiting execution. There may be within this death row one or more 'death cells', special units in which the condemned person is kept for a period of hours or a few days immediately prior to the imposition of the sentence.[20]

Death Row Prisoner

A death row prisoner is a prisoner sentenced to death and is normally segregated from other convicts serving fixed terms of imprisonment.[21]

Dignity

The etymological root of dignity is the Latin word '*dignitas*' translated as 'worth'.[22] Dignity is 'a kind of intrinsic worth that belongs equally to all human beings'.[23]

Situating the Death Penalty within Theories

In 1812, a Philadelphia journalist said that 'So much has been written and said on the subject of capital punishments that it seems almost like presumptive vanity to pursue the topic any further. Even after two and a half centuries of moral debate and four decades of constitutional argument, the one thing that seems indisputable is that the death penalty produces an endless stream of discourse'.[24] Four concepts, namely, prison, prisoners, punishment and dignity were explored. Prisons as 'total', 'complete and austere institutions' highlights the symbolic structure of the prison. Prisoners are confined in the physical

20 Schabas, William. *The Death Penalty as Cruel Treatment and Torture: Capital Punishment Challenged in the World's Courts*. Boston, MA: Northeastern University Press, 1996.

21 Ibid.

22 Statman, Daniel. 'Humiliation, dignity and self-respect'. *Philosophical Psychology* 13, no. 4 (2000): 523–40.

23 Gewirth, Alan. 'Human dignity as the basis of rights', in Meyer, Michael J. and William Allan Parent, eds. *The Constitution of Rights: Human Dignity and American Values* Ithaca, NY: Cornell University Press, 1992: 10–4; cited in Knowles, Helen J. 'A dialogue on death penalty dignity'. *Criminology and Criminal Justice* 11, no. 2 (2011): 115–28.

24 Quoted in *Orlando News*, 25 October 2006; cited in Garland, David. *Peculiar Institution: America's Death Penalty in an Age of Abolition*. Cambridge, MA: Harvard University Press, 2010.

space of prisons after confronting the criminal justice system. They, as a social category underscore the concepts of 'marginalised' and 'ghettoised'. The sociology of the punishment highlights concepts such as imprisonment, torture and solitary confinement and the death penalty. Dignity is a cross-cutting issue in these three concepts of prison, prisoners and punishment.

Prisons

Goffman is one of those theorists who articulated the concept of prison while articulating the concept of 'total institution'.[25] Prison is one of the five types of total institutions. It is organised to protect the community against what are thought to be intentional dangers to it and in this kind of total institution the welfare of the persons sequestered is not the immediate issue. In a total institution, all aspects of life are conducted in the same place and under the same single authority. Each phase of the member's daily activity is carried out in the immediate company of a large batch of others in a tight schedule and all are treated alike and are required to do the same thing together.[26]

Baltard coined the term 'complete and austere' for prisons.[27] Foucault explains this through the principles of prison. The first principle of prison is the isolation of the convict from the external world, from everything that motivated the offence, from the complicities that facilitated it and finally the isolation of the prisoners from one another. The second principle of prison is that work alternates with meals and accompanies the convict to evening prayers. The third principle of the prison is that it goes beyond the mere deprivation of liberty and becomes increasingly an instrument for the modulation of the penalty through the execution of the sentence. It is thus a form of social and political control for wider society and not just an institution which controls crime and criminal behaviour.[28]

Prisons are visible embodiments of society's decision to punish criminals.[29] The expurgatory function of prisons also lies in its capacity to remove

---

25 Hacking, Ian. 'Between Michel Foucault and Erving Goffman: Between discourse in the abstract and face-to-face interaction'. *Economy and Society* 33, no. 3 (2004): 277–302.

26 Goffman, Erving. 'On the characteristics of total institutions', in Walter Reed Army Institute of Research: *Symposium on preventive and social psychiatry*. Washington, DC: U.S. Government Printing Office, 1957: 43–84.

27 Foucault, Michel. *Discipline and Punish: The Birth of the Prison*. New York: Vintage, 1977.

28 Ibid.

29 Travis, Jeremy. 'Invisible punishment: An instrument of social exclusion' in Mauer, Marc and Meda Chesney-Lind, eds. *Invisible Punishment: The Collateral Consequences of Mass Imprisonment*. New York: The New Press, 2002: 15–36.

unproductive and disruptive people from the community while its symbolic function lies in its capacity to stigmatise criminality. In a diversionary sense, the prison keeps a focus on crime and the ordinary criminal whilst diverting the gaze away from the harm being done by more powerful members of society. In essence the 'success' of prisons lies in their ability to ensure that its subjects will return to its walls, thus ensuring its continued existence.[30] Prison is merely a response to crime but originated to challenge the social crisis during the eighteenth century on how prison presented a vision of control and functioned to establish a morality of law and order.[31] A prison is in effect a reserved *space* which serves to forcibly confine a legally denigrated *population* and wherein this latter evolves its distinctive *institutions*, culture and sullied identity. It is thus formed of fundamental constituents of stigma, coercion, physical enclosure and organisational parallelism and insulation that make up a ghetto and for similar purposes. The prison cleanses the social body from the temporary blemish of those of its members who have committed crimes. Thus it forms an 'urban condom' and like Durkheim states, individuals who have violated the socio-moral integrity of the collectivity by infringing on '*definite and strong states of the collective conscience*'.[32]

In India, prisons constitute the largest part of penal administration. European prison systems were instituted in Asia and Africa as an important component of colonial rule. In India, for example, the English prison system was introduced during the second half of the eighteenth century, when jails were established in the regions of Calcutta and Madras.[33] India is a federation; the state's functions are distributed structurally into the central and state subjects. Jails and prisons are essentially state subjects. Prisons continue to be located and structured more or less as they were in colonial times. Any change that has been made has been incorporated somewhat clumsily into the old system that basically served the triple colonial aims of order, economy and efficiency.[34] Today there are 1,391 prisons of various types which house over three times the population of offenders. The system is structured as follows: There are 130

---

30 Garland, David. *Punishment and Modern Society: A Study in Social Theory*. Chicago, IL: University of Chicago Press, 1993.

31 Ignatieff, Michael. *A Just Measure of Pain: The Penitentiary in the Industrial Revolution*. London: Macmillan, 1978.

32 Wacquant, Loïc. 'The new "peculiar institution": On the prison as surrogate ghetto'. *Theoretical Criminology* 4, no. 3 (2000): 377–89.

33 Davis, Angela Y. *Are Prisons Obsolete?* New York: Seven Stories Press, 2003.

34 Singh, Hira. 'Prison administration in India: Contemporary issues', in Shankardass, Rani Dhavan, ed.Punishment and the Prison: Indian and International Perspectives. New Delhi: Sage, 2000: 112–22.

central prisons, 346 district prisons, 780 sub-jails, 19 women prisons, 53 open jails, 21 borstal schools, 38 special schools, four other jails.[35]

Prisoners

The social and economic groupings in society are not evenly represented in the prison populations. In most countries one can discover that, invariably, a disproportionate number of prisoners come from minority groups. For instance in Australia they are Aboriginals; in New Zealand, Maori; in Central Europe, Romas (otherwise known as Gypsies).[36] This focus grew alongside the development of theories pertaining to theorists documenting the changing socio-economic, political and historical conditions that have led to mass incarceration. The concern about large number of prisoners behind bars centres on the necessity to move the analysis beyond death row prisoners to the state that incarcerates these marginalised and socially excluded groups. In doing so, it highlights the dark underbelly of prison regimes which imprisons the socially marginalised.[37]

In the 1860s it was reported that there were 211 executions carried out from 1865 to 1869 in India. Of these 20 were women. All these executions were for murder specifically that committed in a fit of rage, or with the intention to steal, or jealousy/love/passion, or property issues.[38] The situation or reasons for the crime has not changed much in 2015. Prison statistics in India have demonstrated that the vast majority of prisoners behind bars are from the socially marginalised population with no education, no occupation and from utterly poor backgrounds. They also represent social inequalities in terms of belonging to the lower caste in the dominant caste system of India. A total of 129,608 convicts were reported under various terms of sentences in the country at the end of 2013. There were 382 prisoners on death row accounting for 0.3% of the total convicts. Uttar Pradesh has reported the highest number of such death row prisoners (82), followed by Karnataka (43), Maharashtra (41), Bihar (39), Delhi (30), Madhya Pradesh (29), Gujarat (18) and Haryana (11).[39] Unlike last prison statistics, there is a bifurcation of women prisoners on death row. Of the 382 prisoners, 10 are women prisoners on death row. The death penalty

---

35 National Crime Records Bureau. Prison Statistics India 2013. See http://ncrb.gov.in/ (last accessed 28 November 2014).

36 Coyle, Andrew. *Understanding Prisons*. Maidenhead: Open University Press, 2005.

37 Wacquant. 'The new "peculiar institution": On the prison as surrogate ghetto'.

38 Mouat, Frederic John. 'On prison statistics and discipline in lower Bengal'. *Journal of the Statistical Society of London* 25, no. 2 (1862): 175–218.

39 National Crime Records Bureau. Prison Statistics India 2013. See http://ncrb.gov.in/ (last accessed 28 November 2014).

is a system of raw power. For political outsiders such as women and minorities, it carries with it a ripple effect that expands through their whole experience. Women prisoners walk a boundary that they have no power to draw. Despite their sparse number, women on death row are powerful prisoners of the state and social expectations of womanhood and their very existence defines us all.[40]

Punishment

Punishment is awarded in various forms – imprisonment, torture, solitary confinement and capital punishment. It is a 'complex set of interlinked processes and institutions rather than a uniform object or event'. It is identified as the key to developing moral standards and argues that locking up offenders condemns the offence and reinforces society's values.[41] It is a known fact through the work of Foucault and Marx that punishment is a raw exercise of power. But it is also an expression of moral community and collective sensibilities, in which penal sanctions are an authorised response to shared values individually violated.[42] The goals of punishment are deterrence, retribution, rehabilitation or public protection and it does not explain why societies punish or why punishments take the forms they do.[43]

The idea of punishment as the purpose of imprisonment is plain enough – the person who has committed a wrong or hurt must suffer in return.[44] Imprisonment or incarceration is a legal punishment that may be imposed by the state for the commission of a crime or disobeying its rules. The objective of imprisonment varies in different countries and may be punitive. The other objectives of imprisonment are for incapacitation, deterrence and rehabilitation and reformation.[45] The emergence of imprisonment as the characteristic penal sanction in modern society can be explained by the prison's role in a wider network of disciplinary institutions and practices designed to govern individuals for a variety of purposes. Imprisonment thus provides a level of reassurance

40 Carroll, Jenny E. 'Images of women and capital sentencing among female offenders: Exploring the outer limits of the eight amendment and articulated theories of justice'. *Texas Law Review* 75 (1996): 1413–52.

41 Garland. *Punishment and Modern Society*.

42 Garland, David. 'Sociological perspectives on punishment'. *Crime and Justice* 14 (1991): 115–65.

43 Colvin, Mark. *Penitentiaries, Reformatories and Chain Gangs: Social Theory and the History of Punishment in Nineteenth-Century America*. New York: St. Martin's Press, 1997.

44 Sykes, Gresham M. *The Society of Captives: A Study of a Maximum Security Prison*. Princeton: Princeton University Press, 1958.

45 Scott, Charles L., ed. *Handbook of Correctional Mental Health*. Washington, DC: American Psychiatric Publishing, 2009; cited in Lyons, Lewis. *The History of Punishment*. London: Amber Books, 2003.

to the community that something is being done about crime.[46] The 'pains of imprisonment' are the loss of liberty; the deprivation of goods and services; the frustration of sexual desire; the deprivation of autonomy and the deprivation of security.[47]

Torture as punishment was used to extract confessions in the thirteenth century as a consequence of the revival of the Roman Law and the example of the Catholic Inquisition. Great Britain had supposedly replaced judicial torture with juries in the sixteenth century, yet torture still took place there in the sixteenth and the seventeenth centuries in cases of sedition and witchcraft. Punishment in the colonies not surprisingly followed the patterns established in the imperial centre.[48] India was a colony of the British till her independence in 1947. Even after independence the main penal laws such as the Indian Penal Code, 1860; the Code of Criminal Procedure, 1973; The Indian Evidence Act, 1872 and many others from the colonial times are still retained in India. Some of the provisions in these laws are termed as 'draconian or black laws'. Though India is guided by the world's largest constitution which spells out the Fundamental Rights of its citizens, none of the laws or the Constitution of India has either defined torture, nor prohibited torture in the penal laws.

In India, the methods of torture used in detention range from beatings on the soles of the feet and all body parts, deprivation of food, water and sleep; the application of electric shocks to sensitive body parts; submersion under water; the insertion of needles under the nails; suspension from the ceiling; the rolling of heavy weights across the body; burning with cigarette butts; insertion of chillies, chilli powder and other painful materials into the rectum and many other forms of mutilation and pain-inducing treatments. Rape and other forms of sexual abuse are common forms of torture. Regular reports appear in the Indian media of the stripping and parading of women as a punishment for crimes. Many individuals have died as a result of injuries sustained during torture and, aside from the psychological trauma that is sometimes undergone by victims of torture; many individuals suffer permanent physical damage, including renal failure, blindness, paralysis and impaired use of limbs as a result of the treatment they have undergone in detention.[49] The purpose of torture is not only to make one talk, but to betray others too. The victim must turn oneself in by one's screams and submission into a lower animal, in the eyes of

---

46 Duff, R. Antony and David Garland, eds. *A Reader on Punishment.* Oxford: Oxford University Press, 1995.

47 Sykes. *The Society of Captives.*

48 Hunt, Lynn. *Inventing Human Rights: A History.* New York and London: Norton, 2007.

49 Ghosh, Srikanta. *Torture and Rape in Police Custody: An Analysis.* Delhi: Ashish Publishing House, 1993.

all and in one's own eyes.[50] In the course of torture, the victim loses reference to the world where one is thrown back to one's bodily existence. The victim thus gradually loses one's human voice. At the end, one can but scream like an animal, or only just breathe and stutter.[51]

Solitary confinement is one of the oldest and most enduring prison practices. It is the physical isolation of individuals who are confined to their cells for 22 to 24 hours a day.[52] Barring the death penalty, it is also the most extreme penalty which can legally be imposed on prisoners. Solitary confinement was first widely and systematically used with the aim of reforming convicts. However rather than being reformed, many prisoners became mentally ill. Such criticisms led to the dismantling of the isolation system in most countries by the late nineteenth century; however solitary confinement had become a permanent feature of prison systems world-wide. It was used mainly as a form of short-term punishment for prison offences, for holding political prisoners, for protective custody and as a technique for 'softening-up' detainees, particularly those suspected of crimes against the State, before and between interrogation sessions.[53] Meaningful contact with other people is typically reduced to a minimum. The reduction in stimuli is not only quantitative but also qualitative. The available stimuli and the occasional social contacts are seldom freely chosen, are generally monotonous and are often not empathetic.[54]

Towards the end of the twentieth century and at the beginning of the twenty-first, the use of long term, large scale solitary confinement returned in the form of 'supermax' (short for super-maximum security) and 'special security' prisons. Paradoxically, although prison overcrowding is a major issue in many jurisdictions, the use of various forms of solitary confinement has increased in the last two decades.[55] It is used in the context of the 'war on terror'; as disciplinary punishment; with pre-trial detainees, the mentally ill and death row prisoners and, in the so-called 'supermax' prisons.[56] Indian Supreme

---

50 Sartre, Jean-Paul. 1958. Preface in Alleg, Henri. *The Question*. Bison Books, 2006.

51 Scarry, Elaine. *The Body in Pain: The Making and Unmaking of the World*. New York: Oxford University Press, 1985.

52 Nowak, Manfred. *Torture and other Cruel, Inhuman or Degrading Treatment or Punishment* A/63/175 See http://daccess-dds-ny.un.org/doc/UNDOC/GEN/N08/440/75/PDF/N0844075.pdf?OpenElement (last accessed 25 March 2015).

53 Shalev, Sharon. 'A sourcebook on solitary confinement'. London: Mannheim Centre for Criminology, London School of Economics and Political Science, 2008. See http://solitaryconfinement.org/uploads/sourcebook_web.pdf (last accessed 31 July 2015).

54 Nowak. *Torture and other Cruel, Inhuman or Degrading Treatment or Punishment*.

55 Shalev. 'A sourcebook on solitary confinement'.

56 Nowak, Manfred. Foreword in Shalev, Sharon. 'A sourcebook on solitary confinement'.

Court judgments say that solitary confinement is an isolation of the prisoner from other co-prisoners and complete segregation from society. It further acknowledges that it is an extreme measure and is to be rarely invoked in exceptional cases of unparalleled brutality and atrocity.[57]

Historically, one of the most strikingly obdurate forms of social control has been capital punishment – taking the life of the accused offender. Its ancient heritage can be traced back through England, Greece and ancient Babylon to the Code of Hammurabi, which listed 25 different capital crimes. These crimes included disobedience to parents, adultery, blasphemy, violations of the Sabbath, incest and witchcraft.[58] In modern times, demands that governments should 'crack down' on offenders are reproduced in the 'tough on crimes' discourse and translated into harsher penalties, comprehensive and punitive community reporting and stringent release plans.[59] The retaliatory law such as capital punishment aims to assuage popular outrage, reassure the public and restore the credibility of the system, all of which are political rather than penological concerns.[60]

In India, death penalty is executed by means of hanging. The prisoner could simply be hanged with a noose, which would then cause the fracturing of the neck. Various prison manuals stipulate on how a hanging should be conducted. For instance in the Maharashtra prison manual, prior to the execution, the Superintendent should see that the rope is carefully tested. It prescribes that as a rule, a bag of sand weighing one and a half times the weight of the prisoner is to be hanged and dropped between 1.830 and 2.440 metres. This action will afford a safe test of the rope. Two spare ropes for each prisoner sentenced to death shall be kept ready in reserve on the scaffold in the event of accidents. This manual also states that if orders are received from the Government that publicity shall be given to the execution of any prisoners, then the Superintendent should inform the District Magistrate and an announcement should be made, 'A.B. convicted of the murder of ... ... was hanged on .... at .... Jail. Let all evil minded persons take warning'. This manual has many provisions such as the confinement of the prisoner; articles to be given when the prisoner comes

57 Munuswamy v Unknown (1947) 1 MLJ 336; Kishore Singh Ravinder Dev v State of Rajasthan, AIR 1981 SC 625.

58 Loeb, Robert H. and George F. Cole. *Crime and Capital Punishment.* New York: F. Watts, 1986; cited in Wilcox, Norma and Steele, Tracey. 'Just the facts: A descriptive analysis of inmate attitudes toward capital punishment'. *The Prison Journal* 83, no. 4 (2003): 464–82.

59 Pratt, John. *Governing the Dangerous: Dangerousness, Law and Social Change.* Sydney: Federation Press, 1997.

60 Garland, David. *The Culture of Control: Crime and Social Order in Contemporary Society.* Chicago, IL: University of Chicago Press. 2001.

on death row; guarding of the cells of death row prisoners; the procedure for appeals and details of executing a prisoner.[61]

Dignity

Dignity is a concept which intersects with the concepts of prison, prisoners and punishment. This leads us to the discussion on dignity especially in the context of capital punishment. The constitutive elements of dignity are the 'minimum core' characteristics of 'being human', notably the singularity of each human being, the equality of all human beings and the personal autonomy necessary to live a dignified life.[62]

Historical accounts of human dignity typically distinguishes four different sources: the Greek and Roman heritage culminating in Cicero's notion of '*dignitas*': the biblical conception of man and woman as being created in the image of God; Kant's *Würde* as opposed to price and, finally, the concept of dignity that turned up after 1945 in numerous declarations and constitutional laws. Although not unrelated, at first sight these traditions point in quite different directions.[63] An analysis of dignity may begin with its etymological root, the Latin '*dignitas*' translated as 'worth'. Thus, when the United Nations (UN) Charter refers to the 'dignity and worth' of a human being, it uses synonyms for the same concept. Other UN instruments speak of 'inherent dignity', an expression that is close to 'intrinsic worth'.[64] The most commonly accepted understanding of dignity is the one that depicts it as an inalienable element of humanity, without which a person ceases to have any worth – physical, psychological, or moral. A person is nothing without his/her dignity. Thus dignity is 'a kind of intrinsic worth that belongs equally to all human beings'.[65]

In this context, it is also imperative to understand the relationship between human dignity and human rights. In several documents we find the idea that human dignity is the basis of human rights.[66] Human dignity is seen as only another label for 'the entire set of human rights'; the difference would just be a linguistic one. In this sense human dignity would be violated if the most

61 Maharashtra Prison Manual, 1978. (Chapter 'Prisoners sentenced to death').

62 Gewirth. 'Human dignity as the basis of rights', cited in Knowles, Helen J. 'A dialogue on death penalty dignity'.

63 Kaufmann, Paulus, Hannes Kuch, Christian Neuhaeuser and Elaine Webster, eds. *Humiliation, Degradation, Dehumanization: Human Dignity Violated*. Library of Ethics and Applied Philosophy, Vol. 24. Dordrecht: Springer, 2010, pp. 1–6.

64 Statman. 'Humiliation, dignity and self-respect'.

65 Gewirth. 'Human dignity as the basis of rights', cited in Knowles, Helen J. 'A dialogue on death penalty dignity'.

66 Universal Declaration of Human Rights, 1948 (Articles 21 and 23).

fundamental liberties and rights were at stake and is understood as 'the right to have rights'. It would not just be another name for the entire set of human rights, but possessing human rights would be the normative consequence of having human dignity. The foundational function in relation to human rights is central to this concept of human dignity. In this context, the normative consequences of human dignity would have to be explained in terms of human rights.[67]

If we want to understand human dignity, we should start with instances of its violation, instead of attempting to derive a conception of human dignity from our normative ethics as Kant did. We should choose a *negative approach*, i.e. start from situations which we are inclined to describe as violations of human dignity. Then we should ask ourselves what is it that makes it so appealing to use this concept instead of referring to, for example, harming, infringing autonomy or violating human rights. The negative turn, i.e. to start with violations, not only provides us with a philosophical motivation to look into human dignity but also gives us an idea of which features may be essential for human dignity.[68]

The concept of dignity with its negative violation can be understood when people are tortured in detention or custody. In torture, it is not the intensity of the pain or suffering inflicted, but the powerlessness of the victim and the purpose for which the pain is being inflicted. Powerlessness means that the victim is under the direct control of the torturer; this usually means detention or a similar form of deprivation of personal liberty.[69] It is the experience of absolute powerlessness which creates the feeling among the victims of certain gross human rights violations, to have lost their dignity and humanity.[70] Furthermore, an Indian Supreme Court judgment holds that custodial torture is a naked violation of human dignity and degradation which destroys to a very large extent human personality.[71]

An intimate connection exists between the notion of human dignity and the notion of humiliation.[72] Humiliation is seen as first and foremost an injury to the dignity of its victims, an injury usually described in figurative language:

---

67 Kaufmann et al. *Humiliation, Degradation, Dehumanization.*

68 Ibid.

69 Nowak, Manfred. 'What practices constitute torture? US and UN standards'. *Human Rights Quarterly* 28, no. 4 (2006): 809–41.

70 Nowak, Manfred. Foreword in Kaufmann, Paulus et al., eds. *Humiliation, Degradation, Dehumanization: Human Dignity Violated.* Library of Ethics and Applied Philosophy, Vol. 24. Dordrecht: Springer, 2010: v–vi.

71 D. K. Basu v State of West Bengal – AIR (SC)-610, 1997-SCC-1–416.

72 Statman. 'Humiliation, dignity and self-respect'.

in humiliation, one 'is stripped of one's dignity'[73] one is 'robbed of' dignity,[74] or simply 'loses' it.[75] If there is no concept of human dignity, then there is no concept of humiliation either.[76] Techniques such as the stripping of detainees, terrifying them into fouling themselves and sexually taunting them, epitomise the loss of dignity that accompanies deliberate humiliation.[77] That is why the experience of being degraded, devalued, unattractive, 'not worth bothering with', is so threatening for humans, an experience common to both shame and humiliation.[78] A strong feeling for feeling humiliated exists when the humiliating behaviour is explicitly intended to degrade its victims.[79]

In case of torture, the connection is with terrifying and 'breaking' the victim. Fear is perhaps the most important evil-maker connected with the pain of torture. The torture victim never knows whether one's torturer will do even worse things, regardless of any legal restrictions; the uncertainty is perpetual. Terror itself is closely connected with humiliation, especially when someone else sets about terrifying us. Terror makes us whimper and beg; it makes us lose control of our bowel and bladder. The Abu Ghraib dog handlers had contests to see who could make a detainee foul himself (most of the detainees were men) first. The strategic use of terror is one way that torture and humiliation are tightly bound together. But that is not all. The experience of acute pain is itself degrading because it collapses our world and reduces us to mere prisoners of our bodies. Pain forcibly severs our focus on anything outside of us; it shrinks our horizon to our own body. This is degrading in itself, but when it happens in front of spectators, the experience is doubly shameful and humiliating.[80]

The concept of 'dignity' is an omnipresent component of debates about capital punishment. It is a 'vague but powerful idea'[81] that influences and defines the direction of the death penalty dialogue, in no small part because its vagueness and power enable it to be invoked in support of myriad different

---

73 Gilbert, Paul. 'The evolution of social attractiveness and its role in shame, humiliation, guilt and therapy'. *British Journal of Medical Psychology* 70, no. 2 (2011): 113–47.

74 Dillon, Robin S. 'Self-respect: Moral, emotional, political'. *Ethics* (1997): 226–49.

75 Margalit, Avishai. *The Decent Society*. Cambridge: Harvard University Press, 1996.

76 Ibid.

77 Luban, David. 'Human dignity, humiliation and torture'. *Kennedy Institute of Ethics Journal* 19, no. 3 (2009): 211–30.

78 Gilbert. 'The evolution of social attractiveness and its role in shame, humiliation, guilt and therapy'.

79 Statman. 'Humiliation, dignity and self-respect'.

80 Luban. 'Human dignity, humiliation and torture'.

81 Dworkin. *Taking Rights Seriously*; cited in Knowles, Helen J. 'A dialogue on death penalty dignity'.

views. There has been a lot of deliberation on death penalty as a form of torture.[82] At a basic level, any kind of punishment is morally problematic because it involves applying punitive measures to certain individuals, measures which society deems immoral if applied to anyone else. If every human being has dignity and is equal – insofar as they automatically possess dignity by virtue of being human – then surely an individual's dignity is threatened by differential treatment. Differential treatment that is punitive – and, as such, is undesirable to the recipient – enhances the threat to dignity. In this respect, there can be no greater punitive act of indignity than an execution. Humans have such dignity regardless of how they are treated; certain modes of treatment may violate but not remove their dignity.[83] This is indeed true, but ends when the 'treatment' in question is capital punishment.[84]

The late Justice Krishna Iyer, the Indian Supreme Court Judge was very vocal about the barbarity of the death sentence and said that it is an inviolable command of compassionate culture and fundamental expression of social justice grandeur. No civilised state shall have the authority to inflict the death penalty even in the rarest of rare cases, lest it be condemned as guilty of barbarity and devoid of humanity. Universal respect for human rights demands the absolute abolition of capital punishment as no state committed to social justice and human rights can stultify or demolish the right to life of any human being.[85] The death penalty degrades human dignity because it cannot be shown to serve any penal purpose more effectively than a significantly less drastic punishment. The 'paradigm violation' of human dignity is 'torturous punishment', which capital punishment is, mentally more than physically.[86] Thus it is that the infliction of severe pain which is immoral, is a great immorality committed by the state.[87]

---

82 Camus, Albert. *Reflections on the Guillotine.* Indiana: Fridtjof-Karla Publications, 1960; Bluestone, Harvey and L. Carl McGahee. 'Reaction to extreme stress: Impending death by execution'. *The American Journal of Psychiatry* 119, no. 5 (1962): 393–6; Nowak, Manfred. *Torture and other Cruel, Inhuman or Degrading Treatment or Punishment.*

83 Gewirth. 'Human dignity as the basis of rights', cited in Knowles, Helen J. 'A dialogue on death penalty dignity'.

84 Knowles, Helen J. 'A dialogue on death penalty dignity'. *Criminology and Criminal Justice* 11, no. 2 (2011): 115–28.

85 Iyer, Krishna V.R. 'Capital punishment: A penological barbarity' *Mainstream* XLV, no. 45 (2007). See http://www.mainstreamweekly.net/article394.html (last accessed 31 July 2015).

86 Furman v Georgia 408 U.S. 238 (1972).

87 Kateb, George. *Human Dignity.* Cambridge, MA: Harvard University Press, 2011.

Legal Framework of Death Penalty in India

In India, the Supreme Court has restricted the use of the death penalty in the 'rarest of rare' cases which means that the crime committed should be so heinous that it disturbs the collective conscience of the community.[88] This phrase of 'collective conscience' was introduced by Durkheim as a label for 'the totality of beliefs and sentiments common to the average members of a society'.[89] The judgment further states that when a crime is an extremely brutal, grotesque, diabolical, revolting or dastardly manner so as to arouse intense and extreme indignation of the community, then it becomes the rarest of rare. Indian law provides for all requisite procedural safeguards. Juvenile offenders cannot be sentenced to death under any circumstances and there are specific provisions for pregnant women. Death sentences in India must also be confirmed by a superior court. The President of India in all cases and the Governors of States under their respective jurisdictions, have the power to grant pardons, reprieves, respites or remissions of punishment or to suspend, remit or commute the sentence of any person convicted of any offence.[90]

The Constitution of India symbolically attaches importance to international legal obligations when it exhorts to endeavour to 'foster respect for international law and treaty obligations in the dealings of organised peoples with one another'.[91] India has refused to sign any Optional Protocols to Human Rights Conventions or the Rome Treaty establishing the International Criminal Court which have international enforcement mechanisms that go beyond mere reporting by the state. It has not signed the Second Optional Protocol to the International Covenant on Civil and Political Rights, 1989.[92] This protocol aims at the abolition of the death penalty. India has also not ratified the Convention

88 Bachan Singh v State of Punjab, 2 SCJ 474 (1980); AIR 1980 SC 898; AIR 1982 SC 1325; 1 SCR 145 (1983).

89 Durkheim, Emile. *The Division of Labor in Society*. Trans. G. Simpson. New York: Macmillan, 1933.

90 Human Rights Council, *National Report submitted in accordance with paragraph 5 of the annex to Human Rights Council Resolution 16/21* – India, A/HRC/WG.6/13/IND/1, para. 28. See http://daccess-dds-ny.un.org/doc/UNDOC/GEN/G12/116/85/PDF/G1211685.pdf?OpenElement (last accessed 25 March 2015).

91 The Constitution of India, 2007 (Article 51).

92 General Assembly Resolution 44/128, *Elaboration of a second optional protocol to the International Civil and Political Rights, aiming at the abolition of the death penalty*, A/RES /44/128 See http://www.un.org/documents/ga/res/44/a44r128.htm (last accessed 25 March 2015).

against Torture and Other Cruel, Inhuman or Degrading Treatment or Punishment (CAT), 1984.[93]

The provisions relating to capital punishment are embodied in the Indian Penal Code, 1860 and the Criminal Procedure Code, 1973. The Indian Penal Code, 1860 is the substantive law, which suggests the offences which are punishable with death sentence. It provides capital punishment for eight categories of offences namely – waging war against the Government of India; abetting mutiny by a member of the armed force; fabricating false evidence with the intent to procure conviction of a capital offence, with the death penalty applicable only if an innocent person is in fact executed as a result; murder; murder committed by a life convict; abetting the commission of suicide of a child or insane person; attempted murder actually causing hurt, when committed by a person already under sentence of life imprisonment; kidnapping and dacoity (banditry) with murder.[94]

Committing any act using unlicensed firearms or explosives that results in death, is punishable by death.[95] Engaging in organised crime, if it results in death, is also punishable by death.[96] Committing, or assisting another person in committing *Sati* (the burning or burying alive of widows or women) is also punishable by the death penalty.[97] Bearing false witness in a capital case against a member of a scheduled caste or tribe, resulting in that person's conviction and execution, carries the death penalty.[98] Terrorism-related offenses resulting in death are punishable by death.[99] Terrorism-related offenses not resulting in death by use of any special category explosive to cause an explosion likely to endanger life or cause serious damage to property is punishable by the death penalty.[100] Furthermore, a recent law on rape not resulting in death states that a person who in the course of a sexual assault inflicts injury that causes the victim

---

93 General Assembly Resolution 39/46, *Convention against Torture and Other Cruel, Inhuman or Degrading Treatment or Punishment* A/RES/39/46 See http://www.un.org/documents/ga/res/39/a39r046.htm (last accessed 25 March 2015).

94 Indian Penal Code, 1860 (Section 121, 132, 194, 302, 303, 305, 307, 364(a) and 396).

95 The Unlawful Activities (Prevention) Amendment Ordinance, 2004 (Article 6).

96 Maharashtra Control of Organised Crime Act, 1999 (Article 3); Karnataka Control of Organised Crime Act, 2000 (Article 3); Andhra Pradesh Control of Organised Crime Act, 2001 (Article 3).

97 The Commission of Sati (Prevention) Act, 1987 (Article 4).

98 Indian Prevention of Atrocities Act, 1989 (Section 3 (2)(i)).

99 Terrorist and Disruptive Activities (Prevention) Act of India, 1993 (Article 3, 28, 43); Prevention of Terrorism Act of India, 2002 (Article 3(2)(a)).

100 Explosive Substances (Amendment) Act, 2001(Section 3).

to die or to be left in a 'persistent vegetative state' is punishable by death and that repeat offenders of gang rape are also punishable by death.[101]

Also drug trafficking not resulting in death where an individual who has been convicted of the commission of, attempt to commit, abetment of, or criminal conspiracy to commit any one of a range of offenses related to drug trafficking (e.g. trafficking of cannabis and opium) commits another offense related to the production, manufacture, trafficking, or financing of certain types and quantities of narcotic and psychotropic substances, s/he can be sentenced to death.[102] A recent Bombay High Court found that the mandatory imposition of the death penalty under the Narcotic Drug and Psychotropic Substances Act, 1985 violated the Right to life of the Constitution of India,[103] and ruled that it be changed to give judges a discretionary choice of punishment. Offences related to the enemy and punishable with death includes an exhaustive list of offences that could be committed by armed force personnel. Military offenses not resulting in death if committed by a member of the Army, Navy, or Air Forces, are punishable by death: committing, inciting, conspiring to commit, or failing to suppress mutiny; desertion or aiding desertion; cowardice; treacherous acts; committing or inciting dereliction of duty; aiding the enemy; inducing individuals subject to military law not to act against the enemy; imperilling Indian or allied military, air, or naval forces in any way.[104] The Indian Parliament also approved legislation making acts of terrorism aimed at sabotaging oil and gas pipelines punishable by death, in cases where the act of sabotage is likely to cause the death of another person. During the same time the western state of Gujarat passed a law that the production and sale of toxic alcohol shall be punishable by death.[105]

The Criminal Procedure Code, 1973 is a comprehensive law that sets out procedural rules for the administration of criminal justice. It is the main legislation on procedure for administration of substantive criminal law in India, thus it also explains the procedure to be followed in death penalty cases. The Criminal Procedure Code, 1973 was the result of a major overhaul of the previous Code of Criminal Procedure, 1898. The Criminal Procedure Code, 1973 made the death sentence an exceptional punishment and required that

---

101 Criminal Law (Amendment) Act, 2013 (Section 9).

102 Narcotics Drugs and Psychotropic Substances Act of India, 1985 (Article 31A).

103 The Constitution of India, 2007 (Article 21).

104 The Air Force Act of India, 1950 (Section 34, 37, 38, 46); Indo-Tibetan Border Police Force Act, 1992 (Section 16, 19, 20).

105 Amnesty International Report 'Death sentences and executions 2011' London. Index number: ACT 50/001/2012 See https://www.amnesty.org/en/documents/ACT50/001/2012/en/ (last accessed 25 March 2015).

judges record 'special reasons' where they did not award life imprisonment.[106] This was a clear statement from the legislature that the death penalty is now an exceptional punishment while life imprisonment would be the obvious punishment for murder. The wellspring of law in India is 'The Constitution of India' which, in turn, gives due recognition to statutes, case law and customary law consistent with its dispensations.

With regards to custodial torture and dignity, Indian Supreme Court has condemned the tyrannical way of custodial interrogation that exposes the suspect to the risk of abuse of his person or dignity and that interrogation should not be accompanied with torture or the use of third degree methods.[107] The Indian Evidence Act, 1872 also states that a confession to a police officer cannot be proved as against a person accused of any offence and confession caused by threats from a person in authority in order to afford any evil of a temporary nature would be irrelevant in criminal proceeding.[108] The Indian Penal Code, 1860 provides for punishment to one who voluntarily caused hurt or grievous hurt to extort confession or any information which may lead to detection of an offence or misconduct.[109]

Guidelines for Awarding Death Sentence

In India the mandatory death penalty has not been in existence since at least 1860, except for a very limited class of offenders. In 1983 the Supreme Court of India struck down a mandatory death sentence on the basis that no judicial discretion existed for the offence concerned e.g. murder committed whilst under a life sentence.[110] The murders are 'terrible' and therefore, the fact of the murder being 'terrible' cannot be an adequate reason for imposing the death sentence, otherwise death sentence becomes a rule, not an exception and therefore the law which states that, 'When the conviction is for an offence punishable with death or, in the alternative, with imprisonment for life or imprisonment for a term of years, the judgment shall state the reasons for the sentence awarded and, in the case of sentence of death, the special reasons for such sentence'[111] becomes a dead letter.[112]

106 The Code of Criminal Procedure, 1973 (Section 354(3)).
107 Kartar Singh v State Of Punjab 1994 SCC (3) 569, JT 1994 (2) 423.
108 Indian Evidence Act, 1872 (Section 24).
109 Indian Penal Code, 1860 (Section 330 and 331).
110 Mithu v State of Punjab (1983) AIR 473, 1983 SCR (2) 690.
111 The Code of Criminal Proçedure, 1973 (Section 354(5)).
112 Sant Gopal Alias Bhagat v State of U.P., 1995 CriLJ 312.

The Supreme Court evolved with the doctrine of 'rarest of rare' crimes in Bachan Singh vs State of Punjab 1980.[113] In the following years, the below propositions were made in the Machhi Singh And Others vs State Of Punjab.[114]

1. The extreme penalty of death need not be inflicted except in the gravest cases of extreme culpability;
2. Before opting for the death penalty the circumstances of the 'offender' are also required to be taken into consideration along with the circumstances of the 'crime';
3. Life imprisonment is the rule and death sentence is an exception. In other words the death sentence must be imposed only when life imprisonment appears to be an altogether inadequate punishment with regard to the relevant circumstances of the crime and provided the option to impose sentence of imprisonment for life cannot be conscientiously exercised with regard to the nature and circumstances of the crime and all the relevant circumstances;
4. A balance-sheet of aggravating and mitigating circumstances has to be drawn up and in doing so the mitigating circumstances have to be accorded full weighting and a just balance has to be struck between the aggravating and the mitigating circumstances, before the option is exercised.

The Supreme Court further says that in order to apply these guidelines inter alia the following questions may be asked and answered:

1. Is there something uncommon about the crime which renders a sentence of imprisonment for life inadequate and calls for a death sentence?
2. Are the circumstances of the crime such that there is no alternative but to impose the death sentence even after according maximum weightage to the mitigating circumstances which speak in favour of the offender?

Machhi Singh And Others v State Of Punjab held that the 'rarest of rare' requirement is satisfied when the 'collective conscience' of the community has been 'shocked' and when the balance sheet of aggravating and mitigating circumstances indicates that a sentence of life imprisonment would be 'inadequate' because it would denigrate the seriousness of the crime. However

113 Bachan Singh v State of Punjab, 2 SCJ 474 (1980); AIR 1980 SC 898; AIR 1982 SC 1325; 1 SCR 145 (1983).

114 Machhi Singh And Others vs State Of Punjab 1983 AIR 957, 1983 SCR (3) 413.

in 1996, in a decision of the Supreme Court in *Ravji v State of Rajasthan*,[115] the Bachan Singh dictum of 'rarest of rare' was ignored. The judgment of Ravji said that 'it is the nature and gravity of the crime but not the criminal, which are germane for consideration of appropriate punishment in a criminal trial'. Two accused were given the death sentence based on this reasoning. Seven cases that followed relied on Ravji's case; leading to 13 convicts being sent to death row without applying the Bachan Singh dictum for determining the sentence. In 2009, the court found in other judgments that Ravji's judgment was in contravention of the law.[116]

Thus death sentences in India are handed over on the basis of 'rarest of rare' crimes which are those crimes which disturb the conscience of the society. Often the conscience of the society is reflected in public opinion. Bachan Singh case also states that judges should not take upon themselves the responsibility of becoming oracles or spokesmen of public opinion. It further states that it is often better, not being representatives of the people, as a matter of judicial restraint, to leave the function of assessing public opinion to the chosen representatives of the people in the legislature concerned.[117]

Possible Judicial Stages in Case of Death Penalty

The court structure in India is pyramidal in nature. Unlike the American model of dual court system, federal and state, India has a single monolithic system. Hence, the Supreme Court is the highest Apex Court and its verdicts are final in the constitutional matters, customs and tradition and earlier decisions of the various courts.[118] The designations of courts are derived principally from the Code of Civil Procedure, 1908 and the Code of Criminal Procedure, 1973 further embellished by local statutes. These statutes also provide for their functions and jurisdiction.

The Criminal Procedure Code, 1973 provides for the possibility of a three-stage judicial process. The first stage is the trial court stage. Since all death penalty cases involve a charge of murder or other similar serious offences, all initial trials under the ordinary criminal law are held before a District and Sessions Court which are trial courts in a particular state. In the event of the trial court awarding a death sentence, it is mandatory for the respective High

115 Ravji @ Ram Chandra v State Of Rajasthan 1996 AIR 787, 1996 SCC (2) 175.

116 Bariyar v State of Maharashtra 6 S.C.C. 498 (2009); Dilip Tiwari v State of Maharashtra, (2010) 1 SCC 775; Rajesh Kumar v State (2011) 13 SCC 706.

117 Bachan Singh v State of Punjab, 2 SCJ 474 (1980); AIR 1980 SC 898; AIR 1982 SC 1325; 1 SCR 145 (1983).

118 Jois, Mandagadde Rama. *Legal and Constitutional History of India.* Vol. 1. Universal Law Publishing Co, 1984.

Court of that state to confirm the sentence. The High Court has the power to direct further inquiry to be made or additional evidence to be taken upon any point bearing on the guilt or innocence of the accused at this stage. Based on its assessment of the evidence on record, the High Court may: (i) confirm or pass any other sentence, or (ii) annul the conviction and convict for any other offence that the Sessions Court might have convicted the accused of or order a new trial on the basis of the amended charge, or (iii) acquit the accused person. The High Court is also the first appellate court for a person sentenced to death. In the event that a trial court acquits an accused in a case involving a crime punishable by death, the state alone can file an appeal against acquittal before the High Court. The High Court can either confirm the acquittal or set aside the acquittal and convict the accused for the alleged crimes and impose sentence. If the acquittal is set aside and a death sentence imposed, then it provides for an automatic appeal to the Supreme Court. Appeals may also be filed by the state for enhancement of sentence imposed by the trial court or the High Court if it feels that the sentence imposed is inadequate. Ordinarily, relatives of the victims of the crime can file revision petitions (but not appeals) seeking enhancement of the punishment in the High Court or Supreme Court.[119]

The third stage is the Supreme Court. There is no automatic right of appeal from the order of the High Court to the Supreme Court in death penalty cases except in a situation in which the High Court has imposed a death sentence while quashing a trial court acquittal. 'Special Leave' to file an appeal with the Supreme Court has to be granted by the High Court or the Supreme Court has to give leave to file an appeal before it. In the case of some special legislations such as the Terrorist and Disruptive Activities (Prevention) Act 1987, the law provides that appeals against the ruling of the trial court should automatically lie only with the Supreme Court (though this Act lapsed in 1995, trials under this Act continue to this day). The Supreme Court can dismiss a death sentence case *in limine*, i.e. at the threshold stage itself without even admitting the appeal for consideration.

Once the appeal process has been exhausted and the Supreme Court has confirmed the defendant's death sentence, the defendant can submit petitions for mercy to the state or national executive.[120] According to the Indian Constitution, the State Governor and the President of India both have the

---

119 The Code of Criminal Procedure, 1973 (Section 366, 367, 378, 377).

120 Amnesty International India and People's Union for Civil Liberties (Tamil Nadu and Puducherry) 'Lethal lottery: The death penalty in India – A study of Supreme Court judgments in death penalty cases 1950–2006', 2008. Index number: ASA 20/007/2008 See https://www.amnesty.org/en/documents/ASA20/007/2008/en/ (last accessed 25 March 2015); The Constitution of India, 2007 (Article 72); Indian Penal Code, 1860 (Section 432, 433).

power to suspend, pardon, or commute death sentences.[121] With the advice of their cabinets, these individuals can pardon those on death row.[122] In addition, the President can commute the death sentence of any offender to any other punishment provided by the Penal Code without the consent of the offender.[123] However, if the President rejects the mercy petition, then a 'black warrant' is issued to the convict which states the date of execution. To avoid what happened to Afzal Guru and Ajmal Kasab in terms of not being able to inform their families, a recent judgment stated that the families should be informed and prisoners should know about their execution 14 days in advance.[124]

In early 2014 the Indian Supreme Court upheld that the President had to consider mercy petitions within a reasonable time period. The Court upheld that inordinate, undue and unreasonable delay in considering mercy petitions constitutes torture in violation of Indian and international law. It also went on to issue certain guidelines when considering mercy petitions. The Court stated that prisoners have a right to legal aid to prepare legal challenges to the clemency process and to be informed of the result of their mercy petition in writing. In addition, it stated that prison officials should ensure that prisoners receive regular mental health evaluations and be given 'appropriate medical care'.[125]

Fundamental Rights of Condemned Prisoners

Even a person under death sentence has human rights which are non-negotiable and even a dangerous prisoner, standing trial, has basic liberties which cannot be bartered away. Convicts are not, by mere reason of the conviction, denuded of all the fundamental rights which they otherwise possess. A compulsion under the authority of law, following a conviction, to live in a prison house entails to, by its own force, the deprivation of fundamental freedoms such as the right to move freely throughout the territory of India or the right to 'practice' a profession. The convict is entitled to the precious right guaranteed by Article 21

---

121 The Constitution of India, 2007 (Article 72).

122 Utkarsh, Anand., 'SC admits PIL, will look into review of Presidential pardon'. *The Indian Express* See http://archive.indianexpress.com/news/sc-admits-pil-will-look-into-review-of-presidential-pardon/1196646/ (last accessed 24 March 2015).

123 Indian Penal Code, 1860 (Section 54); Amnesty International India and People's Union for Civil Liberties (Tamil Nadu and Puducherry) 'Lethal Lottery: The Death Penalty in India – A study of Supreme Court judgments in death penalty cases 1950–2006', 2008. Index number: ASA 20/007/2008. See https://www.amnesty.org/en/documents/ASA20/007/2008/en/ (last accessed 25 March 2015).

124 Shatrughan Chauhan & Another v Union of India & Others, Judgment, Writ Petition No. 55 of 2013, Supreme Court of India, Jan. 21, 2014.

125 Shatrughan Chauhan & Another v Union of India & Others, Judgment, Writ Petition No. 55 of 2013, para. 259(8), Supreme Court of India, Jan. 21, 2014.

of the Constitution that s/he shall not be deprived of her/his life or personal liberty except according to procedure established by law.[126]

Housing death row convict is a challenge to the state. Confinement inside a prison does not necessarily import cellular isolation. Segregation of one person all alone in a single cell is solitary confinement. The Indian Penal Code, 1860 prescribes the limit of solitary confinement.[127] Since it is a separate punishment, the Court alone can impose it. It would be a subversion of this statutory provision in the Indian Penal Code to impart a meaning to a section of the Prisons Act, 1894 which states that, 'Every such prisoner under sentence of death shall be confined in a cell apart from all other prisoners and shall be placed by day and by night under the charge of a guard'.[128]

Provisions Regarding the Stay of Death Sentence Prisoners

When a prisoner is sentenced to death the Criminal Procedure Code, 1898 provided for hanging by the neck till death.[129] This was not amended by the Criminal Procedure Code, 1973 and it read, 'When any person is sentenced to death, the sentence shall direct that he be hanged by the neck till he is dead'.[130] The jail manual of each state provides a chapter on death penalty convicts. For instance a particular jail manual provides for the various steps leading to the execution of the death sentence. It states that every prisoner under the sentence of the death should immediately on her/his arrival in the prison after sentence, be searched by, or by order of the Deputy Superintendent and all articles should be taken from her/him which the Deputy Superintendent deems it dangerous or inexpedient to leave in her/his possession. Furthermore, it states that every such prisoner should be confined in a cell apart from all other prisoners and should be placed under the charge of a guard day and night. After such admission of the prisoner in the jail, the Deputy Superintendent is required to examine the cell and has to satisfy her/himself that it is secure and has no article which can be used as a weapon or instrument with which the prisoner can commit suicide.[131] It goes on further to describe the various restrictions pertaining to the use of the apparels, bedding, constant surveillance of the guard, how to keep the keys of the cell 'safe', that at no other time should the door of the cell in which a condemned prisoner is confined be opened without

126 Bhuvan Mohan Patnaik v State of Andhra Pradesh, 2 SCR 24: AIR 1974 SC 2092 (1975).

127 Indian Penal Code, 1860 (Section 73 and 74).

128 Prisons Act, 1894 (Section 30 (2)).

129 The Code of Criminal Procedure, 1898 (Section 368(1)).

130 The Code of Criminal Procedure,1973 (Section 354(5)).

131 Jail Manual of Punjab and Haryana (Chapter XXXI, Para 847 (1) and (2)).

first handcuffing the prisoner and so securing her/him against the possibility of using violence or, if s/he declines to be handcuffed, unless at least three members of the establishment are present so on and so forth.[132]

Review of Literature

There is a vast amount of literature available when it comes to the topic of the 'death penalty' however; there are not many books which are specific to the Indian context. Some of the recent books highlight the issue of death penalty in India. Hood and Hoyle deals with death penalty worldwide with specific reference to India and they also focus on the judgments related to death penalty.[133] These judgments deal with various aspects such as: the delay in deciding the mercy petition; the post mortem to be held after hanging to determine whether hanging was really an acceptable method of execution; informing the family of death row prisoners before their execution,[134] and the undue delay causing death row phenomenon.[135] Similarly, the book by Johnson and Zimring gives an overview of the death penalty in Asia with reference to retentionist countries, the political conditions of these countries and trends in death penalty. There is no particular chapter dedicated to India however, there is an appendix which has information about death penalty in terms of jurisprudence and the patterns that are evident in the executions in India. It further discusses the role of the courts and executive clemency in terms of judicial executions in India.[136]

Hood and Deva discuss human rights, politics and public opinion with reference to the death penalty in Asia. Three out of fourteen chapters in this book discuss the issue of death penalty in India. In one of the chapters, Bindal and Raj Kumar discuss the legal, constitutional and human rights dimension on the abolition of the death penalty. They situate their argument by contextualising the 'rarest of rare' doctrine. They use the term '*jurispathic*' derived by Cover. It refers to the behaviour of judges which is the violent tendencies of judges in their very interpretive act of upholding the death penalty. Because of the

---

132 Law Commission of India: 187th Report on 'Mode of Execution of Death Sentence and Incidental Matters', October 2003.

133 Hood, Roger and Carolyn Hoyle. *The Death Penalty: A Worldwide Perspective.* Oxford: Oxford University Press, 2014.

134 Shatrughan Chauhan & Another v Union of India & Others, Judgment, Writ Petition No. 55 of 2013, Supreme Court of India, Jan. 21, 2014.

135 Triveniben v State of Gujrat, (1988) 4 AScc 574; (1989) 1 SCC, 678.

136 Johnson, David T. and Zimring, Franklin E. *The Next Frontier: National Development, Political Change and the Death Penalty in Asia.* Oxford: Oxford University Press, 2009.

violence they command, judges characteristically do not create law but kill it.[137] They also emphasise the dissenting judgment that Justice Bhagwati gave in case of Bachan Singh. Justice Bhagwati quite categorically mentioned that the death penalty is unconstitutional as it violates Article 14, 19 and 21 of the Constitution of India.[138] They also discuss the *Shifting Sands* of 'rarest of rare' where they provide examples of cases which did or did not receive the death penalty. They made an attempt to reconceptualise the debate on death penalty with new perspectives. They also provide an excellent argument on the 'lack of remorse' on the prisoner's face when taken for trial. This is a concept that has often been highlighted in death penalty cases where the media, prosecutors and judges point out the 'lack of remorse' on the accused person's face. They finally make a case for the abolition of death penalty on the lines of constitutional and human rights discourse.[139]

Deva provides a critique on the doctrine of 'rarest of rare' by analysing 86 cases (January 2000 to October 2011) decided by the Indian Supreme Court. He discusses the contentious reasons such as shaking the conscience of the nation; dictating to the lower court what crimes come under 'rarest of rare' (for example, honour killing); lack of adequate reasons or analysis when handing over death penalty. The Supreme Court in the Bachan Singh case mentions that the judge has to draw a balance sheet when handing out this punishment. Further Deva brings in an important argument for upholding the death sentence in India. It is in the context of the offender's rehabilitation possibility and he cites that Indian courts do not have access to relevant information to make a risk assessment in individual cases.[140] Besides he says that in the absence of such crucial information as well as the lack of a system to collect such information,

---

137 Cover, Robert M. *Narrative, Violence and the Law: The Essays of Robert Cover.* Edited by Martha Minow. Ann Arbor: University of Michigan Press, 1995; cited in Bindal, Amit. and Raj C. Kumar. 'Abolition of the death penalty in India: Legal, constitutional and human rights dimension', in Hood, Roger and Surya Deva, eds. *Confronting Capital Punishment in Asia: Human Rights, Politics and Public Opinion.* Oxford: Oxford University Press, 2013, pp. 123–40.

138 Article 14 states: The State shall not deny to any person equality before the law or the equal protection of the laws within the territory of India; Article 19 states: Everyone has the right to freedom of opinion and expression, this right includes freedom to hold opinions without interference and to seek, receive and impart information and ideas through any media and regardless of frontiers. ; Article 21 states: No person shall be deprived of his life or personal liberty except according to procedure established by law.

139 Bindal, Amit. and Raj C. Kumar. 'Abolition of the death penalty in India: Legal, constitutional and human rights dimension', in Hood, Roger and Surya Deva, eds. *Confronting Capital Punishment in Asia: Human Rights, Politics and Public Opinion.* Oxford: Oxford University Press, 2013, pp. 123–40.

140 Bariyar v State of Maharashtra 6 S.C.C. 498 (2009).

courts should be reluctant to impose the death penalty. He concludes that the principle of awarding the death penalty in the 'rarest of rare' cases has outlived its utility and that the application of the 'rarest of rare' guidelines of *Bachan Singh* is applied quite inconsistently and in an arbitrary fashion. They provide analysis of various judgments discussing the arbitrariness of these two concepts that are applied in cases where the death sentence is awarded.[141] In some cases, where the crime is similar, some are awarded death sentence, some are not. Similarly, 'Lethal lottery' is a report which analysed Supreme Court judgments in India from 1950 to 2006. This again was a study which deliberated on the jurisprudence of death penalty and was not an empirical study.[142]

In the same book edited by Hood and Deva, Batra writes about the death row phenomenon and on India's 'Delay' jurisprudence. He discusses the limitations in various cases referring to the death row phenomenon in India.[143] His contention is that unlike international jurisprudence on the broader issue of the death row phenomenon, Indian jurisprudence is limited to the time on death row due to a delay by the executive in the disposal of mercy petition. Further he highlights the 'capital gridlock' a term used by Johnson and Zimring.[144] The discussion by Johnson and Zimring centres around the traffic created at the gridlock due to lack of execution. Similarly, Batra compares Indian's virtually declining execution and the traffic formed thereof causing a 'capital gridlock' of people waiting to be executed.[145]

Among other publications in India, it is Balagopalan who questions the validity of the death penalty and states that it has no place in a civilised society. He has compiled articles, petitions and campaign statements on the death

141 Deva, Surya. 'Death penalty in the 'rarest of rare' cases: A critique of judicial choice-making', in Hood, Roger and Surya Deva, eds. *Confronting Capital Punishment in Asia: Human Rights, Politics and Public Opinion*. Oxford: Oxford University Press, 2013, pp. 238–86.

142 Amnesty International India and People's Union for Civil Liberties (Tamil Nadu and Puducherry) 'Lethal lottery: the death penalty in India – A study of Supreme Court judgments in death penalty cases 1950–2006', 2008. Index number: ASA 20/007/2008 See https://www.amnesty.org/en/documents/ASA20/007/2008/en/ (last accessed 25 March 2015).

143 Triveniben v State of Gujrat, (1988) 4 AScc 574; (1989) 1 SCC, 678; Sher Singh and Others v State of Punjab AIR 1983 SC 465; 1983 SCR (2) 582, 591.

144 Johnson and Zimring. *The Next Frontier*.

145 Batra, Bikramjeet. 'Don't be cruel … : The "death row phenomenon" and India's "delay" jurisprudence', in Hood, Roger and Surya Deva, eds. *Confronting Capital Punishment in Asia: Human Rights, Politics and Public Opinion*. Oxford: Oxford University Press, 2013, pp. 287–312.

penalty in India.[146] Most books discuss only the concept of 'rarest of rare' from the Bachan Singh Case.[147] Schabas discusses abolition of the death penalty in international law. He deliberates on the United Nations' Human Rights System, International Humanitarian Law, European Human Rights Law and Inter-American Human Rights Law, African Human Rights Law and International Criminal Law. With regards to India, Schabas mentions Bachan Singh like most other books but makes a comparison with Article 6 of the International Covenant on Civil and Political Rights, 1989 on the right to life. He also relates that mandatory sentencing to death is unconstitutional with regards to this particular case.[148]

In one of the chapters on state killing in India, in the book edited by Sarat and Boulanger, Eckert[149] states very briefly about civilised killing which is death penalty and mentions the legal provisions under which one is awarded the death penalty in India. However in most of the chapter, she discusses encounter killings or extrajudicial killings in India which she calls 'The Illegitimate Sibling of Capital Punishment'. Hence, there is not much information on the death penalty in this book.[150] In the book edited by Scherdin, Batra provides an analysis of the legal and institutional framework within which death penalty operates in India. Further he questions the gaps in the clemency process. Even though he admits that staying in the prison till death as an alternative to death penalty is dubious; he subscribes to this idea because it shows a response to violent crimes at the same time the State would not execute people.[151]

Hodgkinson's edited book gives a good overview and a new perspective on various topics related to death penalty. It has chapters from specific countries: Malawi, Taiwan, Belarus, Afghanistan, Canada, Uganda, Liberia, Romania and Viet Nam. There was no specific chapter on India. However, there are two chapters relevant to this book on the children and families of death row prisoners. Kearney discusses the various researches that have been conducted with this group of children. She mentions that most studies were qualitative

---

146 Balagopal, K. 'Of capital and other punishments'. *Economic and Political Weekly* 33, no. 38 (1998): 2438–47.

147 Hodgkinson, Peter and William Schabas, eds. *Capital Punishment: Strategies for Abolition*. Cambridge: Cambridge University Press, 2004.

148 Schabas, William. *The Abolition of The Death Penalty In International Law*. Cambridge: Cambridge University Press, 2002.

149 Eckert, Julia. 'Death and the nation: State killing in India', in Sarat, Austin and Christian Boulanger, eds. *The Cultural Lives of Capital Punishment: Comparative Perspectives*. Redwood City: Stanford University Press, 2005, pp. 195–218.

150 Sarat, Austin and Christian Boulanger, eds. *The Cultural Lives of Capital Punishment: Comparative Perspectives*. Redwood City: Stanford University Press, 2005.

151 Scherdin, Lill, ed. *Capital Punishment: A Hazard to a Sustainable Criminal Justice System?* Farnham: Ashgate Publishing, 2014.

in nature, given the emotionally-charged and sensitive nature of the work and she suggests some quantitative research that is required in order to seriously address the needs of this neglected population.[152] Furthermore, Kandelia and Hodgkinson draw our attention to the family members of death row prisoners who are lost in the debate on the death penalty. They say that the family members are perceived as being as culpable as the offender and most of them are left to their own device to survive the entire process, including the execution and the aftermath.[153] This is very true, for instance nobody cared for Dhanajoy's family or Afzal Guru's family after their execution. Kandelia and Hodgkinson highlight the contact with family in prisons in United States. It talks of weekly visits where the prisoners are not allowed to touch their family members. In some states, prisoners are chained when they are brought out to meet their family members. It is difficult for both sides to bear the pain and humiliation.[154]

In the edited book by Unnithan, Johnson writes about the death penalty policy of India.[155] Like previous literature in this field, it focuses on the 'rarest of rare' doctrine. The chapter also describes the history of punishment and death penalty in India which stresses the aspect of *ahimsa* (non-violence) in the country's history. It explains how capital punishment was used extensively in colonial India by the British Empire to control its colonial subjects and reinforce its sovereignty. He also provides the history of how capital punishment was given to the lower caste and class. While discussing the low rate of execution in India, he argues that India has serious problems with lethal violence and a large supply of potentially capital cases which combines with an independent and sensational media that forms public opinion. But at the same time, he says that the low rate of execution in India is because of extra-judicial killing which triggers no public outrage. Further he also argues that two institutional actors play a key role in low execution rates. These are the courts and executive clemency. Courts are required to impose capital punishment only in the 'rarest of rare' cases. Hence not many are awarded the death penalty in the first place. Besides, executive clemency is routinely used at the state and national levels to delay executions indefinitely. Moreover, Johnson talks about the culture of

152 Kearney, Helen. 'Children of Parents Sentenced to Death'. Quaker United Nations Office, 2012: 145–66. See http://www.quno.org/sites/default/files/resources/ENGLISH_Children%20of%20parents%20sentenced%20to%20death.pdf.

153 Kandelia, Seema and Peter Hodgkinson. 'The greater stigma? Family visits to the condemned', in Hodgkinson, Peter, ed. *Capital Punishment: New Perspectives*. Farnham: Ashgate Publishing, 2013, pp. 127–44.

154 Hodgkinson, Peter, ed. *Capital Punishment: New Perspectives*. Farnham: Ashgate Publishing, 2013.

155 Johnson, David T. 'The death penalty in India', in Unnithan, N. Prabha, ed. *Crime and Justice in India*. New Delhi: SAGE Publications India, 2013, pp. 365–89.

capital punishment that exists in India. He cites the example of the Machhi Singh judgment that any sentence less than death would 'denigrate' the seriousness of the offense.[156] Johnson finally questions why India needs capital punishment especially when it is inconsistent with her values.

Roadmap of the Book

This book is about exploring whether the dignity of prisoners on death row is upheld after confronting the criminal justice system. It contains four chapters. The introduction in chapter 1 sets the tone of the book while explaining the highs and lows of the research and providing the rationale behind it. It contextualises the research question and its specific objectives. In addition to providing a brief theoretical and legal background to the book, it also highlights the recent literature, with reference to death penalty in India and discusses the scope of the book. Chapter 2 articulates the methodological and ethical concerns. It discusses the methodology with specific reference to methodological interpretation, research design, sampling, data – collection, instruments used for it and data-analysis and limitations of the methods. It further explores the ethical aspects as it deals with human subjects as participants. Chapter 3 describes the prisoners on death row with reference to their demographic profile and the impact of their incarceration on their families. It further elaborates the processes leading to the death penalty, the infrastructure of the prison and death row, the lives of prisoners on death row and the death row syndrome or phenomenon. Chapter 4 synthesises the empirical findings to answer the main research question on dignity of the prisoners on death row. It also states the strengths and limitation of the study. This chapter attempts to summarise the knowledge produced in this research and states the implications of the book.

---

156 Machhi Singh And Others vs State Of Punjab 1983 AIR 957, 1983 SCR (3) 413.

Chapter 2

Articulation of Methods and Ethical Concerns

The prison setting was not alien to me. I worked both as a researcher and social worker in this setting. Thus, I have had dual roles of being a social worker and a researcher which required some amount of distinction. As a researcher, presenting the voices of prisoners came with several challenges. This chapter articulates the methodological framework and its limitations. Further, it articulates the ethical concerns of the study. Finally, it deliberates on the (non) separation of methods and ethics.

Methodological Framework

The study in this book used a qualitative research paradigm to understand the lives of prisoners on death row. Data was collected using semi-structured interview guides from 111 prisoners on death row from 16 prisons across India. The data was analysed using Tesch's method of interpretation. The study was underpinned by the theories of phenomenology and symbolic interactionism. Finally the framework also takes into account the methodological limitations of the study.

Qualitative Research Paradigm

In order to explore the way prisoners on death row experience and perceive their lives, world and make meaning of that, a design which encapsulates their lives was implemented.[1] This approach allowed access to contents that were not anticipated a priori as well as an exploration of the research topic from the standpoint of the research population.[2] The qualitative approach is research about a person's life, lived experiences, behaviours, emotions and feelings as well as organisational functioning, social movements and cultural phenomena.

---

1 Briggs, Charles L. *Learning How to Ask: A Sociolinguistic Appraisal of the Role of the Interview in Social Science Research*. 1st edn. Cambridge: Cambridge University Press, 1986.

2 Silverman, David. *Interpreting Qualitative Data: Strategies for Analyzing Talk, Text and Interaction*. London: Sage Publications Limited, 1993.

The work is interpretive and 'carried out for the purpose of discovering concepts and relationships in raw data and organising these into a theoretical explanatory scheme'. In qualitative research it is not the researcher's perception or perspective that matters, instead it is how the research participant sees events or happenings.[3] Qualitative research design endeavours to elicit the data into findings based on the experiences and perceptions of prisoners on death row.

Instruments used in the Study

The interview guides used in this study drew on narrative and phenomenological frameworks of interviewing. The use of interview guides was productive in facilitating information of the complex subjective experience and perception of the prisoners. Such interviews followed a format which explored both the experience and perception of the prisoners. These were captured with the phenomenological approach of tapping experiences. At the same time this interactive process in a 'total institution' was necessary to understand the meanings of these experiences or perception.[4] I used a semi-structured interview-guide which had closed and open-ended questions.[5] The questions were designed mainly to understand the demographic profile of the prisoners, to record their experiences after the arrest, their experiences in police custody, being produced before the magistrate for the first time, being transferred to judicial custody (prison), their appeal stage, their perceptions and experiences during the trial and finally after being sentenced to death and living on death row. Additionally, there were questions on the perception of the treatment by the criminal justice system in all these situations. There were other actors such as family members, lawyers, judges, magistrates, prison officials, police officers, prison visitors and media personnel in the narration of the prisoners. The main theme of all the questions was related to their perception of dignity. The instrument used for collecting data was tested among friends and colleagues in Vienna because it was not feasible to test the instrument directly in an Indian prison due to time constrains. The questions were prepared with my understanding about the working of the criminal justice system and based on the United Nations Standard Minimum Rules for the Treatment of Prisoners, 1955. Based on general guidelines to ensure that all those being interviewed are subject to similar stimuli and thereby allowing for a common base for data

---

3 Strauss, Anselm and Juliet Corbin. *Basics of Qualitative Research*. 2nd edn. Thousand Oaks, CA: Sage, 1998.

4 Goffman, Erving. 'On the characteristics of total institutions' in Walter Reed Army Institute of Research: *Symposium on Preventive and Social Psychiatry*. Washington, DC: U.S. Government Printing Office, 1957: 43–84.

5 Appendix to this volume: Interview guide for prisoners on death row.

analysis, the semi-structured interview was found to be the most appropriate research tool to achieve the main objective of the study.[6]

Sampling

Table 2.1 below describes the number of prisons for which permissions were received and the actual number of prisons visited. There is a deliberate omission of information on prisoners on death row in each prison as this would lead them becoming identifiable. The highest numbers of prisoners were in Karnataka followed by Maharashtra, Tamil Nadu, Kerala, Punjab and Assam.

Table 2.1 Permission received and actual prisons visited

Sr. No.	Region	State	Permissions received for the number of prisons	Actual prisons visited	Total number of prisoners interviewed
1	Western	Maharashtra	2	2	
2	Northern	Punjab	3	2	
3	Southern	Kerala	2	2	
		Karnataka	2	2	
		Tamil Nadu	7	5	
4	North-Eastern	Assam	3	3	
Total			19	16	111

India is primarily divided into six regions: Central, Eastern, Northern, North-Eastern, Southern and Western region. The initial sampling scheme was to choose one state from each region based on certain criteria such as area, capital, population, language, rate of literacy and sex ratio and the data was to be obtained from the Census Data of India, 2001. The idea was to merge these criteria with prison statistics data. However, I did not receive permission from the states that were selected on the basis of the sampling. On the advice of a colleague, I wrote to all the prisons housing death row prisoners and conducted interviews in the States that granted me permission.

6 Lofland, John. *Analyzing Social Settings: A Guide to Qualitative Observation and Analysis*. Belmont, CA: Wadsworth, 1971.

Data Collection

The total number of prisoners interviewed was 111 prisoners. The prison statistics in that year recorded 186 prisoners on death row.[7] The data was collected from 111 prisoners over a period of five months (February 2011 to August 2011) from 16 prisons based in six different states in India. The permission to interview the prisoners was sought from the Inspector General Prisons or The Ministry of Home Affairs of the particular State. Once the permissions were received, the prison departments were contacted and a time was fixed to interview prisoners. In an effort to ensure consistency across the interview, I facilitated each conversation. The design of the interview was tentative and modified in accordance with new findings – resulting from the flexible way of questioning.[8] This flexibility contributes to the quality and credibility of the interview.[9] I made notes during the interviews with the consent of the participants as no tape-recorder was allowed inside the prison. The interviews were held in various parts of the prison – some on death row, some in the Superintendent's office and some in work sheds and a few in prisons classrooms. Each interview lasted for an average of 25 minutes. Prisoners were encouraged to share their experiences and perceptions than describing their case details. There were four translators who were part of the study – In the State of Assam, Tamil Nadu and Karnataka.

Data Analysis

I adapted Tesch's proposed steps for data analysis. After transcribing the interviews of the prisoners on to Word Document, I grouped them under similar and most-described themes.[10] The themes identified were the following: socio-demographic profile, arrest, police custody, court room experiences, judicial (prison) custody, media, death row, lawyers, family, death sentence, death row phenomenon and dignity. I abbreviated the themes as codes and observed the organisation of data to check if new categories or codes emerged. The aim was to reduce the total list of categories by grouping together co-related topics. Lines drawn between the categories indicated interrelationship of categories. The data belonging to each

---

7 National Crime Records Bureau. Prison Statistics India 2007. See http://ncrb.nic.in/PSI-2011/Full/PSI-2011.pdf (last accessed 2 February 2013).

8 Rubin, Herbert J. and Irene S. Rubin. *Qualitative Interviewing: The Art of Learning Data.* Thousand Oaks, CA: Sage, 1995.

9 Suchman, Lucy and Brigitte Jordan. 'Interactional troubles in face-to-face survey interviews'. *Journal of the American Statistical Association* 85, no. 409 (1990): 232–41.

10 Tesch, Renata. *Qualitative Research: Analysis Types and Software Tools.* New York: Falmer Press, 1990.

category was grouped together correspondingly and the preliminary analysis was performed. Re-coding of the data was done whenever necessary.[11] At the same time, memos were used to record insights, ideas, informal and formal discussions with prison officials, lawyers, judges and family members. I recorded any and all the ideas that emerged, even if they were vague or not well-thought out and each memo was given titles and dates.[12] It is imperative to mention that the waiting period of the prisoners influenced the data largely. The recalling of narratives depended on the stage of punishment they were in. For instance a prisoner who was recently sentenced to death spoke more about the trial and the interaction with the media. In another instance a prisoner on death row for over five or seven years described more about the living death s/he has to undergo each day.

Furthermore, there was a minor quantitative part in the study, where I analysed the demographic profile of the prisoners. It was logical to scrutinise the data quantitatively in terms of age, education, ethnic background, language, education, religion, occupation and the stage of the appeal. This minor quantitative data was analysed using Microsoft Excel. Thus the theoretical position in this study is phenomenology and symbolic interactionism. The method of data collection was the use of semi-structured interviews. Methods of interpretation of the data were qualitative content analysis. Finally, the fields of application were analysis of everyday knowledge.

Methodological Interpretation

The study was guided by the theories of phenomenology and symbolic interactionism. Since the study was concerned with the meanings that the prisoners assign to their situation, dignity and themselves, it drew from the phenomenological approach in an 'attempt to understand the meaning of events and interactions to ordinary people in particular situations'.[13] As a researcher I attempted to gain entry into the world of the prisoners on death row and understand how meaning is constructed about their daily lives. The aim is to examine and clarify human situations, events, meanings and experiences 'as they spontaneously occur in the course of daily life'.[14] Informants who live or have

---

11 De Vos, A.S., Herman Strydom, Christa B. Fouché and C.S.L. Delport. *Research at Grass Roots: For the Social Sciences and Human Service Professions*'. Pretoria: Van Schaik Publishers, 2005.

12 Tesch. *Qualitative Research.*

13 Bogdan, Robert C. and Sari Knopp Biklen. *Qualitative Research in Education. An Introduction to Theory and Methods.* Boston, MA: Allyn & Bacon, 1998.

14 Von Eckartsberg, Rolf. 'Introducing existential-phenomenological psychology', in Valle, Ron, ed. *Phenomenological Inquiry in Psychology: Existential and Transpersonal Dimensions.* New York: Springer, 1998, pp. 3–20.

lived the reality being investigated are recognised as the only legitimate source of data in phenomenological inquiry.[15] Although all qualitative designs call for the researcher to confront the phenomenon under study as much as possible on its own terms,[16] phenomenology takes one step further and the researcher is encouraged to rely on intuition, imagination and universal structures to obtain a picture of the phenomenon.[17] At the same time, phenomenology only provides a 'matrix' for research but cannot itself be based on data.[18] Also it is impossible to access every aspect of the prisoners' experience because a prison setting magnifies the dialectical relationship between the participants (the prisoners) and me (a researcher) instead of promoting a shared perspective and a more egalitarian connection.[19]

Symbolic interactionism makes an entry here. The symbolic interactionist perspective approaches society from the viewpoint of the individual's constitution of meaning in interaction with other individuals. The interaction between individuals takes place in specific situations to which they bring interpretations which are their definitions of the situations. These definitions then direct the interaction process and constitute the reality of the actor (in this case the prisoners).[20] The term symbolic in the phrase symbolic interaction refers to the underlying linguistic foundations of human group life, just as the word interaction refers to the fact that people do not act toward one another but interact with each other.[21] Often, the situation examined is 'exotic'.[22] Such work typically shows little interest in the generalisability of its results, seeing its tasks as giving voice to its research subjects and the description and understanding of

---

15 Baker, Cynthia, Judith Wuest and Phyllis Noerager Stern. 'Method slurring: The grounded theory/phenomenology example'. *Journal of Advanced Nursing* 17, no. 11 (2006): 1355–60.

16 Denzin, Norman K. *Interpretive Interactionism*. Newbury Park: Sage, 2001.

17 Creswell, John W. 'Five qualitative traditions of inquiry', in *Qualitative Inquiry and Research Design: Choosing among Five Traditions*. Thousand Oaks and London: Sage, 1998, pp. 47–72.

18 Luckmann, Thomas. 'Philosophy, science and everyday life', in Natanson, Maurice. *Phenomenology and the Social Sciences*. Vol. 1. Evanston, IL: Northwestern University Press, 1973, pp. 143–86.

19 Kusenbach, Margarethe. 'Street phenomenology the go-along as ethnographic research tool'. *Ethnography* 4, no. 3 (2003): 455–85.

20 Blumer, Herbert. *Symbolic Interactionism: Perspective and Method*. Berkeley: University of California Press, 1986.

21 Denzin, Norman K. 'Symbolic interactionism', in Flick, Uwe et al., eds. *A Companion to Qualitative Research*. London: Sage, 2004, pp. 81–7.

22 Glaser, Barney G. and Anselm L. Strauss. *The Discovery of Grounded Theory: Strategies for Qualitative Research*. New York: Aldine de Gruyter, 1967.

the total particularities of the situation under examination.[23] In the light of the above notions, the synthesis of phenomenology and symbolic interactionism tries its best to accomplish the task of bringing the voices of prisoners. This synthesis acts as a medium to explore if the dignity of the prisoners is upheld, which in turn leads to the description and understanding of the total particularities of the situation.

Methodological Limitations

As in every study, there were a number of methodological limitations. The total sample was 111 prisoners which was quite a representative sample. Based on the Prison Statistics of 2007, there were 186 prisoners on death row.[24] Hence I interviewed 60 per cent of prisoners on death row India as part of the study. However I did not receive permissions from Central or Eastern Indian States. These are states which have the highest number of ethnic minority and lowest literacy rates. Hence samples from these regions would have enhanced the data. There was also a serious lack of updated information on statistics of death row prisoners. For instance, in a particular state the prison statistics of 2007 mentioned 29 prisoners in a particular state but in reality there were over 60 prisoners on death row. I used the prison statistics of 2007 when I began the data collection in February 2011. Further to this, there was only one case-study research which conducted prior to this study. It was interviews of 13 prisoners on death row from Maharashtra.[25] Hence there was no data to fall back on.

In retrospect, the data collection could have been conducted differently. Prisoners could have been asked to fill the closed-end questionnaires on their own. Even though most of the prisoners could not read or write, the ones who could always helped the others. This would have given me more information about prisoner's backgrounds than discussing it with them for the first time. However, it might not be easy to distribute the questionnaire to prisoners as this can be done only in close cooperation with prison officers. At the same time, one has to take into account some inadvertent emergency situation like a custodial death, or an escape from the prison, or illness or a hunger strike by prisoners or when a prisoner decides to climb a tree top and refuses to climb down or perhaps the prison official's foul mood at that time might also be

23 Harris, Scott R. 'What can interactionism contribute to the study of inequality? The case of marriage and beyond'. *Symbolic Interaction* 24, no. 4 (2001): 455–80.

24 National Crime Records Bureau. Prison Statistics India 2007 See http://ncrb.nic.in/PSI-2011/Full/PSI-2011.pdf (last accessed 2 February 2013).

25 George, Reena Mary. Death penalty: A human rights perspective. University of Mumbai, 2009 (unpublished Master's Thesis).

reasons preventing the distribution of questionnaires to prisoners. All of these occurred when I visited the prison.

Furthermore, this study was mainly self-reported data from prisoners who gave interviews. Self-reported data is limited by the fact that it can rarely be verified independently while conducting a qualitative research study and gathering the data on one's own. We have to capture what our participants articulate during the interviews or in questionnaires at face value. There are several potential sources of bias such as selective memory, telescoping, attribution and exaggeration. Selective memory refers to remembering or not remembering experiences or events that occurred at some point in the past. Prisoners have often talked more about being tortured in custody while they forget or do not recall the events such as the first time they are produced in court which happens almost at the same time. Telescoping is recalling events that occurred at one time as if they occurred at another time. Attribution is the act of attributing positive events and outcomes to one's own agency but attributing negative events and outcomes to external forces.[26] Finally, exaggeration is the act of representing outcomes or embellishing events as more significant than is actually suggested from other data. Despite the limitations, it would be interesting to question why prisoners are selective about their memories and why they telescope, attribute or exaggerate certain events.

I was denied access to certain prisoners because of political, security and 'sociological' reasons. One of the reasons was that certain death row prisoners belonged to high profile criminal cases such as terror attacks or serial murders. In one of the prisons, I was only allowed to interview three prisoners who murdered their wives or family members. Since this was a 'sociological' study, according to the prison official's 'logic', only crime related to family was fit for a sociological study. This led me to exclude three women prisoners on death row. I was also not allowed to use recorders during the interview. This was an advantage as well as a disadvantage in terms of methodological reasons. Prisoners would not have trusted a stranger wanting to record their experiences and perceptions. Having no recorder was a means of gaining trust from prisoners. Moreover transcribing 111 recorded interviews in different languages would have been a daunting task. So not having a recorder made data transcribing less difficult. However, there could have been information that I missed jotting down because sometimes prisoners broke down and it would have been insensitive to keep writing notes when the prisoner was crying in front of me.

---

26 Harris, Lois Ruth and Gavin Thomas Lumsden Brown. 'Mixing interview and questionnaire methods: Practical problems in aligning data'. *Practical Assessment Research & Evaluation* 15, no. 1 (2010): 1–19. See http://pareonline.net/getvn.asp?v=15&n=1. (last accessed 31 July 2015).

As with most empirical studies, there was also a longitudinal effect to this study. The time to collect data was simply insufficient. I had to skip going to two prisons in a certain state because they were too distant and I was unable to contact prison officials in that state. I had to return to Vienna because of visa regulations which do not permit an individual to remain out of the country for more than six months. I did not have to go to one of the prisons where I received permission as there was no prisoner on death row. This could have been avoided if there was updated data on prisoners on death row. When I realised that the number of prisoners were not the same as in prison statistics, I asked prison officials about the number of prisoners on death row when I fixed an appointment. This was done so that I could plan my stay in that particular state. They refused this information citing 'security' reasons. Hence planning my stay in a certain state for a number of days relied on the existing data that was available which was as inaccurate as it could be. I received four permissions before I went to India and two while I was in India. In one of these two states, I had to visit the Inspector General's office six times to finally receive my permission to interview three prisoners.

Ethical Consideration

The methodological framework grounds the various ethical concerns that arise in a study. Ethics is a matter of principled sensitivity to the rights of others and being 'ethical' limits the choice we can make in the pursuit of truth.[27] Prisoners are highly vulnerable as research participants and hence it was necessary to be sensitive to the rights of prisoners. Their vulnerability stems from many reasons since the voluntariness of consent may be compromised in prisons. They have severely curtailed freedom and choices and are subject to additional discipline and sanctions by prison guards and officials. Hence prisoners may feel that declining to participate in research is not a feasible option. Moreover, overcrowding and poor access to healthcare may make participation in research seem attractive, without regard to the risks. Since privacy and confidentiality are compromised in prisons, it is likely that the identity of the interview for such a research project may become common knowledge. In this particular study, the group was very clear – death row prisoners. There could also be some information that may lead to embarrassment, stigmatisation, retaliation, or additional punishment. Finally, it is difficult to monitor the adverse events in research conducted in prisons because they are closed institutions. Participants may find it difficult to call attention to problems that arise as a research project is carried out. Prisoners often have other characteristics that

27 Gilbert, Nigel, ed. *Researching Social Life*. London: Sage, 2008.

make them vulnerable, such as poor education, mental health problems and substance abuse problems.[28]

Since prisoners form such a vulnerable population it was also useful to apply ethics on the principles of respect, beneficence and justice.[29] These are basic ethical principles and guidelines from the Belmont Report intended to assist in resolving ethical problems associated with research involving human 'subjects'. The Report refers to the Nuremberg Code which provides for rules intended to guide investigators' appropriate conduct. The principles of ethics describe the rights of the research participants and rights and responsibilities of the researcher. Gilbert says that there are no cut-and-dried answers to many ethical issues which face the social researcher. Very often, rules are inadequate to cover complex situations; at times they come into conflict and they are frequently difficult to interpret or apply. Besides the issues involved are multi-faceted and there are contradictory considerations at play. There is not, necessarily one right and one wrong answer, but this indeterminacy does not mean that ethical issues can be ignored. The best counsel for the social researcher is to be ethically aware constantly.[30] Below are some of the rights of the prisoners and rights and responsibilities of a researcher.

Informed Consent

A very important principle, which is a linchpin of ethical behaviour in research, is the doctrine of informed consent. This states that persons who are invited to participate in social research activities should be free to choose whether to take part or refuse, having been given the fullest information concerning the nature and purpose of the research, including any risks to which they personally would be exposed to, the arrangements for maintaining the confidentiality of the data and so on.[31] The 'irony of informed consent' is that prisoners are nearly powerless and therefore are sometimes coerced into giving this consent. Two of the research participants refused to be interviewed after they were asked for oral consent. All the others were eager to talk to me. Informed consent also

---

28 Lo, Bernard. *Resolving Ethical Dilemmas: A Guide for Clinicians.* Philadelphia: Lippincott Williams & Wilkins, 2009.

29 National Commission for the Protection of Human Subjects of Biomedical and Behavioural Research (NCPHSBBR) (1979) Belmont Report: Ethical Principles and Guidelines for the Protection of Human Subjects of Research, Department of Health, Education and Welfare, Office of the Secretary, Protection of Human Subjects, See http://videocast.nih.gov/pdf/ohrp_appendix_belmont_report_vol_2.pdf (last accessed 10 November 2012).

30 Gilbert. *Researching Social Life.*

31 Ibid.

has to be obtained from the gatekeepers. In this study, the gatekeepers were the prison officials. Even though I received official permission from the Ministry of Home Affairs or the Inspector General of each region, I had to negotiate with the Superintendents for an actual entry into the prison. In many prisons, I was asked to come at a certain time and I was asked to wait outside the prison gates for hours.

For instance, in one of the prisons I travelled to I was made to wait for over two hours and then when I was called 'inside' I was asked to come again the next day. I went outside the prison gate and called the Inspector General of Prisons for that region and explained that I was in India only for a few months, that I have to go to other prisons too and cannot afford to lose days. The Inspector General was kind and asked me to call him back in ten minutes. I did and he asked me to go back to the prison. When I went in to the prison again, the Superintendent told me, 'So, you are now telling the Inspector General Sir that I am harassing you'. I reacted very calmly and explained my situation, that I had not said he was harassing me but that there was a time constraint to my being present in a particular state. He was not friendly to me during the entire process, but I managed to interview three prisoners on that day and the rest of them during the next few days. Another instance asking for permission from gate keepers was this. The officer asked me, 'So why are you so interested in this region which has a high percentage of naxalites? What interest do you have in them?' It is one of the regions in India which is primarily a tribal belt and a stronghold of Naxal groups. I explained to the officer that I was conducting this study in other states in India as well and not just in aforementioned territory. The officer told me, 'Please send us the permission letters from other states and also the reason why you want to conduct the study in this particular region'.

Voluntary Participation

When I went to the prison, there was no question of choosing a sample, it was very clear; everyone on death row in the prison had to be interviewed. When I asked for their consent, two of them refused to be interviewed. However, in one of the prisons, the prison official brought the prisoner back to me and asked me to interview him. I said that if the prisoner does not wish to be interviewed, I would not force him. The prisoner was happy that he did not have to talk to me. He was the only prisoner on death row in that particular prison. He said that, 'You cannot do anything regarding my case hence I do not wish to talk to you'. It was difficult to obtain trust in a short period or have voluntary participation from the prisoners as they have no liberty, are controlled, scrutinised and held responsible by the system for everything they say. Nonetheless all of them participated in the study without being coerced. Also as Wax writes, it would be gross self-deception not to admit that many prisoners talked to me partly because there was nothing more interesting to do.[32]

Anonymity

Anonymisation is a procedure to offer some protection of privacy and confidentiality. Though helpful in the attempt not to identify people, anonymisation cannot guarantee that harm may not occur. How people will react to a research report cannot be foreseen in advance. The context, unless massively disguised, often reveals clues to identify the participants even when names and places are changed.[33] I have written the findings in a way where prisoners or prisons cannot be identified. However, a prison concerned could be revealed with a minute detail such as having a gallows which has to be manually erected. Also, if I mentioned the religious and ethnic details of prisoners on death row, their identities will be revealed even though I anonymise names.

Confidentiality

The common assumption in ethical social science practice is confidentiality in the process of conducting the research and the anonymisation of individuals in report writing. These are often linked because very often it is assumed that since pseudonyms are used in reporting, it justifies the reporting of information obtained in confidence. Most certainly, the two concepts require separate consideration. Confidentiality is a principle that allows people not only to talk in confidence, but also to refuse the publication of any material that they think might harm them in any way.[34] The interviews were to happen in private. However, all the prison manuals state that a prison officer should be present while the interview is conducted. I negotiated with hearing-seeing distance principle – that a prison officer can be at a seeing distance but not a hearing distance.

In one of the prisons, a welfare officer sat right next to me and the prisoner. It was a very small room filled with benches. I told the welfare officer that I cannot interview the prisoner in such a situation where he is overhearing the whole conversation. He said, 'It is the Superintendent's order'. I said, 'No, I cannot continue with the interview'. He said, 'Let us go to the Superintendent'. The Superintendent gave me the most typical answer I have heard in most

32 Wax, Rosalie H. 'Reciprocity in field work', in Adams, Richard N. and Jack J. Preiss, eds. *Human Organization Research.* Homewood, IL: Dorsey, 1960, pp. 90–98; cited in Jackson, Bruce. *Fieldwork.* Urbana: University of Illinois Press, 1987.

33 Gilbert. *Researching Social Life.*

34 Ibid.

prisons, 'You are a woman. These are dangerous men. It is for your security that the officer is sitting next to you'. I replied, 'If it is question of security put me in a bigger room and not in a small room because if the prisoner attacks me or wants to hit me, I cannot run or escape because of the size of the room and this kind officer (pointing to the welfare officer) here will not be able to do a thing to protect me'. They asked me to wait outside for a while and then I was shifted to a bigger room. The officer sat at a 'seeing' distance and not on the same table as me and the prisoner. However, I must admit there were interviews where I could not negotiate this 'hearing-seeing distance' principle. The interview happened in the Superintendent's office where the Superintendent heard the conversation between me and the prisoner. In these cases, I did not ask too many questions. The prisoner spoke themselves about their lives but they knew which information to filter. These interviews were less than 15 minutes.

Data-sharing

The raw data has the identity of each individual. The Raw data of the study was not shared with anyone except with my thesis advisers. This is one of my responsibilities as a researcher to protect and promote the interests and rights of participants. There was also a considerable amount of sensitive information such as experiences of being tortured; the names of police officers who tortured; cases of sexual exploitation of their family members and themselves in many cases and diaries and letters written by prisoners. It is again one of my responsibilities to protect this data so that no harm is caused to the participants. I was asked by certain prison officials to share the data with them but I refused to do that. They did not pressurise me into sharing all the information provided by the prisoners. One of the questions that I was always asked was, 'So tell me, what they told you? Did they tell you about their crime? Do you even know what crime this person has done'?

Non-exploitation and the Upholding of Dignity

It was important that I did not take advantage of my relationship with the prisoners by asking them questions which would cause them further discomfort. During the interviews, none of the prisoners were asked to describe their case. Some of them shared their cases but I never explicitly asked them to do so since documenting details about their cases was not the objective of the study. Furthermore, asking them questions about torture could have given them mental stress. Mostly, all of them spoke about the torture they faced in police custody. The response was that they felt better having a visitor and talking about their lives in the prison as people sentenced to death. Also, when prisoners broke down, there would be a long silence and the conversation began only when the prisoner started talking again. The silences were as important as the narratives. I was not always in a position to protect prisoners from being humiliated. Sometimes I was the cause. For instance, in one of the prisons, I got up to stretch my legs after an hour's interview and took a few steps inside the room where we were conducting the interview. The prison officer yelled at me and said that I was not allowed to walk. I said that I had to stretch my legs after an hour's interview. He did not retaliate against me, but he shouted at all the prisoners who came for the interview thereafter.

Relationship with Participants and other Actors

I was surprised that the prisoners trusted me and spoke openly with me about their experiences. I felt respected with the way each of them dealt with me. Many of them wrote to me and called me from prisons where there is a public phone facility. They informed me about the latest judgments or being on death row. Apart from the prisoners, the relatives of prisoners also called me occasionally to update me about their case status. These members are an indispensable part of the research; they opened their lives and homes to me. I am still in touch with some of them who asked me to gather information about the cases such as checking the Supreme Court website calling their lawyers in order to enquire about the case.

Value Conflicts and Emotions

I was also conscious of the fact that I was a middle-class woman researcher in a setting mainly dominated by men. My relationship with the research participants and gatekeepers was diagonally opposite yet it intersected at some point. There were instances of a conflict of values between me as a researcher and the gatekeepers and prisoners themselves. For example in a conflict with gatekeeper, while waiting at the Inspector General's office of permission, the guards asked me, 'Why do you want to research about death row prisoners; why don't you go research about poor people in the slums? Why are you studying in Vienna if you want to research about prisoners in India?' Another question from prison officials that I regularly faced was, 'Why do you want to talk to the garbage of the society? You are from a 'good' family, why do you want to talk to rapists and murders?' Prison officials also made this statement quite regularly, 'It is because of human rights activists like you that we lose power over them (prisoners) and people like you cause all problems.' I was often perceived as a threat. Another officer told me, 'It is people like you who spoil the society. You want to interview goons and dons who are a menace to the society but you don't want to help the poor out on the streets. Do you know that man is a rapist?'

The value conflicts with prisoners were mainly on trust issues. For instance a prisoner told me, 'How can we tell you about our lives and you say that it will remain confidential? I know that nothing goes out of the prison without the prison official looking at it.' It was difficult to gain the trust of the prisoner and let him know that I did not share the interviews with prison officials. Another conflict of values with prisoners was their perception about research studies. They often told me, 'What is the point in just collecting information if you are not helping us with the case or doing anything about it? Can't you tell the President or others that we are innocent?' Another prisoner told me, 'What you are doing is a complete waste of time and it is total crap.' Sometimes I explained, at times I remained silent. In a prison one of the prisoners told me, 'Madam, please go away, none of us wants to talk to you. We don't trust you.' I stayed behind, talked to two of them who were willing to talk, slowly, I could gain trust and eventually I talked to all the prisoners in that prison. There were quite a few in this one.

Apart from this there are certain other concerns that one might not foresee. These include being a woman researcher, the risk of being incarcerated and relationships with the translators.

Being a 'Woman' Researcher

As a single woman I have been refused accommodation in hotels in Indian towns and cities as they imagined it would be 'dangerous' to give a room to a 'single' woman. It is natural to book a hotel in advance to avoid this problem but there were circumstances where I could not book a hotel in advance. In a particular state I reached the city at night and had not booked a hotel in advance. I went to hotels in the city centre, everyone refused to let me stay as I was a 'single' woman. Finally I had to take accommodation in a five star hotel and they agreed on the condition that I paid the full amount when I registered. I refused and in the end I was allowed to pay the normal advance and full amount when I vacated. There was also an instance where a certain prison officer had my cell phone number as I had to write down information at the security-desk. He sent me 'friendship' text messages/SMS late in the night.

Another problem in an Indian prison setting concerned going to the toilet. The high security yards were far away from the reception area or women's prison. I used to be inside the high security yard from morning till evening; with a break in the afternoon. Prisoners on death row always offered me water or juice and I never refused to drink as it would disappoint them. According to the Indian custom, refusing water from someone shows a lack of respect for the person who offers it. As an outsider, I was not allowed to go on my own anywhere in the prison. Hence when I asked to go to the toilet, there had to be a prison officer or a warder (a trusted convicted prisoner) accompanying me to the women's prison or to the main gate where the toilets were. This meant a loss of time because we walked quite a lot to reach the toilets and at the same time, it was an additional 'job' for the prison officer to make sure that I was safe. Male officers were often surprised when I said that I wanted to go to the toilet. It is not common for Indian women to say 'this' aloud especially to an unknown male. But it is important that one should take care of one's health and not be shy in these situations. Some of the officers even offered me lunch when they saw that I spent hours in the prison without eating. Most of the time, I did not feel threatened by the so-called 'rapists' or 'murderers'. I do not want to hide that there were instances where prisoners tried to intimidate me. I was afraid that I might be attacked. But that was a risk I knew I was taking when I decided to conduct interviews inside a prison. Most of the time, they treated me with much love, affection and respect. Since I stayed from morning till evening in the prison, they offered me water, juice, biscuits and sometimes prison food.

The Risk of Being 'Incarcerated' Quite High in a Prison Study

In most prisons, I had to give an undertaking that no personal information about prisoners will be made public. However, in one of the prisons, I was asked to sign a piece of document already prepared by the prison officer. This paper said that if I 'violate' any rules, the state could take legal actions against me – very much implying that I could be arrested and imprisoned. It did not specify which rules. I refused to sign it. I felt violated and pressurised by the officer to sign it. The officer was angry with me. I told him that I would write a letter reflecting the fact that no personal information will be made public and I wrote on a new sheet of paper that it was my responsibility as a researcher to protect the research participants and make sure that they are not harmed. At this point, I could relate to what prisoners narrated to me during the interviews about being pressurised into signing 'confession letters' which were prepared by someone else.

Working with the Translators

My involvement with translators was manifold. There were four translators in all – three men and one woman. I chose a woman translator to interview the only woman on death row in this particular study. This woman was a contact of the male translator in that particular state. The most significant part of using translators is the risk of biased responses resulting from the use of translators or local research assistants. Also using translators from the same area as the respondent, risks transgressing political, social or economic fault-lines of which the researcher may not be aware.[35] Both these were true in my case. In case of biased responses, a certain prisoner was narrating about the torture in the police lock-up. I wanted to compare the kind of torture practiced in different states in India. Hence I asked the translator to ask, 'Could you please ask if the prison knew of incidences of torture where objects were inserted into private parts?' It was within the flow the interview. The translator looked at me and said, 'How can I ask such a question?' I continued with the interview and asked this question again in the latter part and this time the translator asked it to the prisoners. Similarly, while interviewing the woman prisoner, I asked my translator to ask if she was raped or molested in custody. The translator asked me the same question, 'How can I ask such a question?' But again in the end she asked this to the prisoner. In another instance, the translator started asking questions to the prisoners on his own without translating it to me. This went on for 10 minutes. I asked him, 'So what did he say?' and the translator replied to me in one word about what the prisoner said.

There were situations when instances of transgressing political, social or economic fault-lines occurred. In one of the prisons, we conducted an interview where there was a gang on death row for murdering a group of people. I noticed that the translator was restless during the interview. After the interview, he told me, 'I grew up reading about this case and I told myself, "If I meet this person, I will murder him".' In another instance of value judgment, a prisoner informed us that his mother was an alcoholic. The translator immediately asked the prisoner, 'Your mother drinks alcohol?' This is in line with the value judgment in India that 'good women' do not smoke or drink alcohol. Also the male translator insisted that he should be allowed to translate the interview of the woman prisoner. I refused saying that he could not. He asked me, 'Are you objecting to my translating on your own or are these prison rules?' I said, 'Prison rules do not allow men in a woman's prison but even if they make an exception in your case, I would prefer a woman translator to be able to respect the woman whom we were going to interview'.

(Non)Separation of Methods and Ethics

Often when one talks about 'objective' data or 'pure' science, the human side of a researcher is stashed away. Liebling was asked if she is a criminologist. She said, 'Yes, (but) I am also a human being and any methodological approach

35 Jacobsen, Karen and Loren B. Landau. 'The dual imperative in refugee research: some methodological and ethical considerations in social science research on forced migration'. *Disasters* 27, no. 3 (2003): 185–206.

which asks for separation between these two features of our lives or work is deeply flawed.' Liebling further states that in criminology, the emotional nature of research is hidden, as is the responsibility of the researcher for the effect of one's study on those who participate in it. Prison research is 'emotionally turbulent' and draining. Criminologists like to pretend that this discipline is unsullied by the emotional nature of the research. They are rarely trained to consider the hopes and expectations of their participants and the implications these feelings may have on people's response to the research experience. They tend to present their analysis of the prison in the form of inhuman data. As a result, prison studies have become cold, calculated and surgical – like polished steel. Liebling says that, 'These days, most criminologists make precision cuts – no blood – no humanity. They keep it statistical, inhuman and no compassion.'[36]

Reflexivity that combines subjective emotional feelings with 'objective' data is often seen as unscientific – a premise of positivism roundly criticised by many methodologists. Feminist critics have maintained that feelings, beliefs and values shape research and are a natural part of inquiry. Emotions influence our research and our research can affect us emotionally. Consequently, feminist researchers explore their own research experience, including feelings and emotions, rather than dismissing these as unscientific and irrelevant.[37] Similarly any investigation of other human beings is necessarily a self-investigation as well, because the beliefs and behaviour of one's subjects arouse in the investigator one's own unconscious (and usually infantile) fears, wishes and fantasies. This countertransference phenomenon, a term borrowed from psychoanalytic therapy evokes much anxiety and is extremely painful. For a variety of reasons, related both to the selective recruitment of anthropologists and to the nature of their data, countertransference and its attendant anxieties is especially characteristic of anthropological (sociological) research.[38]

Due to the emotional entanglement with prisoners, my research participants, I was exhausted and distressed with all the information I heard from prisoners about their lives. I was aware from my previous research that it was an emotionally stressful journey but I did not anticipate the magnitude of the emotional stress most likely. During my field work period (February 2011 to August 2011) in

---

36 Liebling, Alison. 'Doing research in prison: Breaking the silence?' *Theoretical Criminology* 3, no. 2 (1999): 147–73; cited in Bosworth, Mary, Debi Campbell, Bonita Demby, Seth M. Ferranti and Michael Santos. 'Doing prison research: Views from inside'. *Qualitative Inquiry* 11, no. 2 (2005): 249–64.

37 Huggins, Martha K. and Marie-Louise Glebbeek. 'Women studying violent male institutions: Cross-gendered dynamics in police research on secrecy and danger'. *Theoretical Criminology* 7, no. 3 (2003): 363–87.

38 Devereux, George and Weston La Barre. *From Anxiety to Method in the Behavioural Sciences*. New Babylon: Studies in Behavioral Sciences 3. The Hague: Mouton, 1967.

India, I had nightmares, gory dreams and I heard voices of prisoners when I closed my eyes. This continued even when I was back in Vienna. Also, in India during the field work, there was no time to debrief or talk to friends. I was travelling from one state to the other. I often fell physically ill during my field work due to the stress. Vomiting and diarrhoea were my constant companions. This would have been due to the long hours spent in the prison, hearing the experiences and transcribing the data at night. Narrations such as a prisoner's wife given electric shock on her nipples and fingers when she was five months pregnant and her eventual death in a hospital made me sick. The execution of Ajmal Kasab (November 2012) and Afzal Guru (February 2013) made me nervous and the nightmares followed. I often woke up having a nightmare about one of my research participants being executed. Another distressing factor was a prisoner whom I had interviewed died in the prison due to 'natural causes'. Another prisoner who was out on parole contacted me via phone and informed me that the deceased prisoner was ill for a long time but was not given any medical care. In Vienna, I could not bring myself to read the raw data in a library which is quiet; it was easier for me to read the raw data and write my analysis in a loud Irish Pub. I could not look at the raw data for at least a month after reaching Vienna. Despite the stress, I did not have the will or the time to go for professional counselling. However, I talked to my university colleagues and debriefed them.

Thus, conducting research in any human environment – particularly in a prison without subjective feeling is almost impossible. The pains of imprisonment are tragically underestimated by the conventional methodological approaches to prison life. Prison is all about pain – the pain of separation and loss, the wrench of restricted contact in the context of often fragile relationships, of human failings and struggles. Garland argues that imprisonment has an expressive or an emotional function. Liebling questions, 'Why is this emotional function of prison so invisible in most empirical research?' The criminal life and the human life that they live, have never been separate, yet many behave, read and write as though they are separate.[39] I was conscious about the invisibility of the emotional function of the prisons in an empirical research. Hence, I tried to give some visibility to this aspect in all chapters. I was privileged to witness human events (death row prisoners) close up and over time, which were privy to community secrets that were generally hidden from the view of outsiders.[40] Hence it was also important for me to present the findings which upheld the principle of respect, beneficence and justice.

39 Liebling, Alison. 'Doing research in prison: Breaking the silence?'

40 Scheper-Hughes, Nancy. 'The primacy of the ethical: Propositions for a militant anthropology'. *Current Anthropology* 36, no. 3 (1995): 409–40.

Chapter 3
'Skipping a Beat': Voices of Prisoners on Death Row

A prisoner on death row merely remains an unrealistic image in most minds because the portrayal of that prisoner comes through various filters such as the media and powerful officials. This chapter aims to create a human picture of prisoners on death row. The demographic profiling of the prisoners enables the creation of such an image. Furthermore, the impact of the incarceration shows the ripples created by the arrest of a prisoner. The modus operandi leading to the death penalty, the basic facilities in the prison and death row are subjects of discussion in this chapter. Finally, the lives of prisoners on death row and death row syndrome or phenomenon are examined to study the situation of the aforementioned.

Demographic Profile of Prisoners on Death Row

The demographic profile of prisoners on death row describes the age, gender, occupation religion, ethnic background, language, education and finally the stages of their appeals. This was carried out with an aim to understand the socio-economic background of the prisoners on death row. Table 3.1 (below) indicates the various demographic profiles.

Age

The age group of prisoners ranged from 18 to 60 years upwards. Maximum number of prisoners (44 per cent) was in the age group of 30–40 years. The longest trial went on for 12 years while the shortest was for 1 year and 2 months. Thus the average number of years a person spent as an undertrial was six years. When the prisoners were arrested, they were very young. Most of them were in their twenties which is also a productive age group. While they were undertrials, they were not allowed to work because only sentenced prisoners were employed. After being on death row, they were left waiting for death in their high security yard and were again not allowed to work. Most of them expressed their discontent over not being allowed to work. The age group 18–40 years amounts to 65 per cent of prisoners which implies that a rather large group of young adults were on death row.

Gender

Almost 99 per cent of the research participants were men. There was one woman whom I interviewed. However, apart from the one woman participant there were other women on death row in India. I was not allowed to interview them in certain states where I had permission or they were in states which were not in my sample.

Occupation

The data indicated that 53 per cent of the prisoners worked as daily wage workers or casual labourers. It reveals that around 15 per cent of the prisoners were unemployed. There were 5 per cent of prisoners who were professionals like engineers, chartered accountants or computer professionals. Around 13 per cent of the prisoners had their own business such as running shops or having upholstery business or electronic shops. Again 14 per cent of the prisoners refused to disclose their occupation.

Religion

Classification of death row prisoners professing different faiths revealed that 67 per cent of them adhered to Hinduism while 14 per cent adhered to Islam. The rest were a minority of Christians, Sikhs and Buddhist (6 per cent, 5 per cent and 2 per cent respectively). Two insisted on putting down their religions as Marxist and Atheist respectively. There was also a small percentage (4 per cent) of prisoners who refused to disclose their religious identity.

Ethnic Background

The Indian caste system has been quite predominant in its diverse culture. Mines describes that *Caste* is derived from a Portuguese term meaning 'colour'. The phrase '*sistemas de castas*' was widely used in the Spanish colonies of the Americas to refer to the different categories of people under the colonial government and their ranking relative to ideas of nobility. In Sanskrit, the term *Varna* also means 'colour' and refers to the textual division of persons into four categories: *Brahman, Ksatriya, Vaisya and Sudra.* The 'untouchables' or the 'dalits' are below these categories. These names are still used by many Indians to designate their general place in a caste-defined society.[1] Almost 37 per cent of the prisoners on death row belonged to the scheduled castes or scheduled tribes or other backward castes. These castes include the *dalits* and certain castes

1 Mines, Diane P. *Caste in India.* Ann Arbor: Association for Asian Studies, 2009.

based on occupation (e.g. oil pressers). The castes were Wadari, Nadar, Jat, Jai Bhim, Bahujan, Banjara Wijai, Ezhava, Lingayatha, Bhovi, Balegera, Ganinga, Kabbariga, Helavagowda and Gowda. Also 44 per cent of prisoners refused to identify the caste they belonged to. The 19 per cent of prisoners who belonged to upper castes came from Karnik, Maratha, Nair, Shafi, Reddy, Shetty, Pujari, Nayak, Kammarareddy and Sunni castes.

Language

India has been a crucible for the drama of language conflict. Some 1500 languages and dialects are spoken by India's 800 million people.[2] Contrary to the state-building efforts in other empires, India remains a linguistic mosaic. No single language stands as the authorised medium for official exchange. Citizens develop complex language repertoires in order to interact with servants, family, merchants, colleagues and officials.[3] In this study, there were prisoners speaking 14 languages. Each of these 14 languages had different dialects. Of these 25 per cent spoke Kannada. This was followed by almost 15 per cent of prisoners speaking Tamil followed by almost 13 per cent speaking Marathi. The other languages were Telugu, Malayalam, Urdu, Punjabi, Assamese, Hindi, Marwadi, Rajasthani and Gujrati. Two of the prisoners also spoke Wadari and Banjara-Gormati. The Wadar of Maharashtra migrated from Andhra Pradesh in the early historical period. They speak among themselves in Telugu and with others in Marathi. The traditional occupation of Wadars is stone-crushing and making stone chips of various forms and sizes.[4] The Banjaras are a class described as nomadic people from the Indian state of Rajasthan, North-West Gujarat and Western Madhya Pradesh and Eastern Sindh province of pre-independence Pakistan. They are also called the 'Gypsies of India'. In Maharashtra, they are called Banjara-Gormati.[5] This Banjaras spoke a language that was spoken only in this community.

---

2 World Development Report 2011, World Bank. See http://siteresources.worldbank.org/INTWDRS/Resources/WDR2011_Full_Text.pdf (last accessed 24 March 2015).

3 Harrison, Selig S. and Karl Wolfgang Deutsch. *The Most Dangerous Decades: An Introduction to the Comparative Study of Language Policy in Multi-Lingual States.* Language and Communication Research Center. New York: Columbia University, 1957; cited in Laitin, David D. 'Language policy and political strategy in India'. *Policy Sciences* 22, no. 3 (1989): 415–36.

4 Singh, Kumar Suresh. *People of India: Maharashtra.* Vol. 30. Mumbai: Popular Prakashan, 2004.

5 Halbar, B.G. *Lamani Economy and Society in change: Socio-cultural Aspects of Economic Change among the Lamani of North Karnataka.* Delhi: Mittal Publication, 1986.

Education

The data indicated that almost 53 per cent of the prisoners had studied up to the tenth grade, which was relatively a low level of education. Of all prisoners on death row, 17 per cent of them were illiterate and have never been to a school or even registered as a child in a school. A relatively small proportion (12 per cent) of prisoners reported that they had completed bachelors, masters, professional degree or vocational training. Again almost 15 per cent of the prisoners refused to disclose their educational level. Some of the prisoners even received part of their education in the prison as undertrials or still continue their education on death row.

Present Stage of Appeal against Death Sentence

This 'present' stage was from the period February 2011–August 2012 which was the period of data collection. The lowest court awarded the punishment for death and the next stage was the High Court which either confirms the verdict of the lower court or commutes it to life or sometimes even acquits the prisoner. More than half of the prisoners' (55 per cent) appeal was in the High Court. The next stage was the Supreme Court which followed the same procedure as the High Court. Around 16 per cent of the prisoners were in this stage of appeal. Once the Supreme Court confirms their death sentence, the next stage is to ask for mercy or clemency or pardon. The Governor of particular states and the President of India are the ones who pardon or give mercy. First it goes to the Governor of the particular state and when the petition is rejected by the Governor, the prisoner has the final gamble to obtain mercy from the President of India. Around 25 per cent of prisoners had their mercy petition before the President of India and/or the Governor of the particular state.

Table 3.1 Demographic profile of prisoners

Characteristics	Category	Results		Total
		Number	per cent	Number
Age	18–29	23	21	
	30–40	49	44	
	41–50	28	25	
	51–60	8	7	
	60 above	3	3	111
Gender	Women	1	1	
	Men	110	99	111

Characteristics	Category	Results		Total
		Number	per cent	Number
Occupation	Daily wage worker/ casual labourers	59	53	
	Business/Own shop	15	13	
	Professional work	5	5	
	Unemployed	17	15	
	Refused to disclose	15	14	111
Religion	Hindu	74	67	
	Islam	17	14	
	Christian	7	6	
	Sikh	5	5	
	Buddhist	2	2	
	Marxist	1	1	
	Atheist	1	1	
	Refused to disclose	4	4	111
Ethnic background	Lower caste	41	37	
	Upper caste	21	19	
	Refused to disclose	49	44	111
Language	Kannada	28	25	
	Tamil	16	14	
	Marathi	14	13	
	Telugu	11	10	
	Malayalam	9	8	
	Urdu	9	8	
	Punjabi	7	6	
	Wadari	6	5	
	Assamese	4	4	
	Hindi	2	2	
	Marwardi	2	2	
	Banjara-Gormati	1	1	
	Gujarati	1	1	
	Rajasthani	1	1	111
Education	Illiterate	19	17	
	1st grade to 4th Grade	11	10	
	5th Grade to 7th Grade	23	20	
	8th to 10th Grade	25	23	
	11th Grade – 12th Grade	4	4	
	Bachelors	6	5	
	Masters	1	1	
	Professional Degree	2	2	
	Vocational training	4	4	
	Refused to disclose	16	14	111
Present Stage	High Court	61	55	
	Supreme Court	18	16	
	Governor	2	2	
	President	25	23	
	Refused to disclose	5	4	111

The Families of Prisoners on Death Row

Several research studies show that incarceration has an impact on the families of prisoners.[6] This was doubled in the case of prisoners on death row.[7] A prisoner on death row said that other convicted prisoners know when they will leave the prison but prisoners on death row do not know when or if at all they will leave the prison. I made a few home visits where it was possible.

Family Impoverished

The prisoners said that often their families had to sell land, houses or gold to pay the lawyer's fees or to provide for daily needs. All the prisoners in this study (except one woman who was a homemaker) were their family's breadwinners. Hence they left their families behind to fend for themselves. One of the prisoners said that his mother comes very rarely to visit him because she does not have the money to travel from the village to the prison. The prisoner said he does not know how his mother feeds herself. He often wonders if his mother has resorted to begging for her survival.

Additionally, prisons are located in areas that are far away from the cities. Prisons are built in 'Locally Unwanted/Undesirable Land Use' (LULU).[8] LULUs can include prisons, dumps, factories, hospitals or asylums. Though LULUs provide community needs it is on the periphery of cities.[9] The distance makes it difficult for families of prisoners to visit them. All prison manual stipulates 20 minutes visiting time. Most families take more than 20 hours to reach the prison. Hence they often bypass the judicial system by paying bribes to the guard in order to spend ten minutes more with the prisoner. A prisoner said that the family had to spend two to three thousand rupees (34–51 Euros approximately) to meet him. This prisoner used a very powerful concept to describe the transition period or the time that has passed by while he was incarcerated on death row. He said that, 'The children are no more half ticket' indicating that

---

6 For example: Western, Bruce and Sara McLanahan. 'Fathers behind bars: The impact of incarceration on family formation'. *Contemporary Perspectives in Family Research* 2 (2000): 309–24; King, Anthony E. 'The impact of incarceration on African American families: Implications for practice'. *Families in Society* 74, no. 3(1993): 145–53; Arditti, Joyce A., Jennifer Lambert-Shute and Karen Joest. 'Saturday morning at the jail: Implications of incarceration for families and children'. *Family Relations* 52, no. 3 (2004): 195–204.

7 Sharp, Susan F. *Hidden Victims: The Effects of the Death Penalty on Families of the Accused.* New Brunswick, NJ: Rutgers University Press, 2005.

8 Martin, R. 'Community perceptions about prison construction: Why not in my backyard?' *The Prison Journal* 80 (2000): 265–94.

9 Popper, Frank J. *Siting LULUs.* Emmitsburg: National Emergency Training Center, 1981.

they would need more money to buy a ticket for a fully-grown child. Since it was very expensive to travel to the prison, visits from the family became infrequent as time passed, thus deepening the divide in the already broken-relationships.

In one of my home visits, the house or rather the hut that the family lived in could have been demolished by heavy rain. The family had a hand-to-mouth existence. They informed me that they often had to take loan from neighbours to go to the High Court which was three hours away from their village. The mother who only spoke a particular language asked me when her son was going to be released. His sister translated it for me in Hindi. I did not have an answer. The news around this prisoner was that he could not be hanged because the state could not find a hangman. A hangman is a person who carries out the execution by pulling the lever to remove the balance from the foot when a person is hanged on a rope. The sister asked if the prison officials had found a hangman. I told her the truth that they had because I had the information from a prison officer that they found a hangman from another city.

Supreme Court Justice Bhagwati states in the famous Bachan Singh case that 'There can be no doubt that the death penalty in its actual operation is discriminatory for it strikes mostly against the poor and deprived sections of the community and the rich and affluent usually escape from its clutches'.[10]

Relatives Dying

Most of the prisoners who were interviewed lost at least one of their parents or relatives during their incarceration. In cases where they knew of the death immediately and wanted to attend the funeral, their bails were rejected. This was during their undertrial period. Their bails were rejected because they were the 'dangerous ones'. In a few cases they could not be informed about the death of the relative because the surviving relatives simply did not have the money to come to the prison to inform them or the letters simply arrived late. According to a very young death row prisoner, the most difficult part of being on death row was that he constantly thought about his parents. One of the prisoners told me that, 'I will commit suicide the day my mother dies'. Another prisoner who was on death row for 10–12 years was crying bitterly and said that it was the first time that someone was talking to him and enquired about his family and so all his 'hidden' grief emerged all of a sudden.

Yet another prisoner mentioned that his mother was 60 years old and father much older than the latter. He used to write letters regularly but there were no replies to the letters so he stopped writing to them. He said that he has not talked to or met his family members for the last two and half years. In another

10 Bachan Singh v State of Punjab, 2 SCJ 474 (1980); AIR 1980 SC 898; AIR 1982 SC 1325; 1 SCR 145 (1983).

home-visit, the day I visited the family, the sister of one of the death row prisoners had died. When asked about the cause of the death, the relatives said that she was ill for a long time but they did not have the money to treat her or admit her in a hospital. The sister who died was survived by a one year old child and an alcoholic husband. I stayed behind for the cremation. The houses that they lived in were in the border of the village. It thus once again proved the social theory of marginalisation that it was the poor and the *dalits* who live in the border of any village or society as they are ghettoised or socially excluded.[11]

One of the other prisoners told me that his mother died and he was informed several days after her death because his relatives did not have the means to travel to a far-away prison. According to him, she died of the burden of his impending death sentence. Yet another prisoner narrated that when his death sentence was confirmed, his father died of grief. His mother was very sick. The frequency of the family visits became less as the years passed by because of abject poverty or deteriorating health. Besides, some of the other reasons for families losing contact with the incarcerated were when the latter murdered their children or wife or when the family feels the stigma of visiting a prison. One of the prisoners said, 'Reena, families visit in the beginning of our incarceration, however as time passes, they get used to the fact that we are not there and in the maximum period of seven years, we lose all contacts.' This was narrated by a prisoner who has been inside for 15 years.

Partners in the (Process of) Leaving

Prisoners on death row have a trial which is 'quite sensational' in the print and the visual media. Hence all the proceedings and stages of the trial were often in the media which became a point of discussion among the relatives according to the prisoners. One of the prisoners said that he was married for three months when he was arrested. After he was given a death sentence, his wife's family forced her to re-marry telling her that her husband will not come back. He said that she wrote a letter to him saying that she will kill herself if she was forced to re-marry. This particular prisoner was a juvenile and in India no person below the age of 18 on the day of crime can be arrested or tried, let alone be on death row. He was eventually released and reunited with his wife. Another prisoner's wife was in the women's section of the same prison. She received a sentence for five years. She cried inconsolably when I met her and said that her husband was innocent. She said that the system could keep him in prison for life if they wanted to but she felt that they should commute his death sentence to life imprisonment.

---

11 Wacquant, Loic. 'Deadly symbiosis when ghetto and prison meet and mesh'. *Punishment & Society* 3, no. 1 (2001): 95–133.

Smaller Children

Children of prisoners form a vulnerable group of individuals who are not recognised as a different group by any of the international or national agencies. One of the prisoners said, 'I have missed the family for an entire generation. It has been over 14 years that I have been in prison and on death row. My daughter shows me photographs during visits. The ones who were babies when I was a free man have babies of their own in their arms. They do not remember me; I do not remember them'.

Another prisoner said that when he was arrested, his wife was pregnant with their third child. He continued that when children came for *mulaquat* (visit), they did not recognise him, especially the younger two. They were of ages – three, five and six. He said that his wife worked in the field as a casual labourer or daily wage worker and earns Rs.25/- per day (40 cents) and because of financial burden they very rarely came for visits. In another case, the prisoner said that when he was arrested he told his father to send his wife away so that she could re-marry and his father informed him that she was pregnant. The prisoner said that he was dumbfounded. This particular prisoner's death sentence was commuted to life and he saw his son when the child was 8 years old.

In cases where the children were a bit older, they were often unable to continue with their education. Prisoners often feel very disappointed that it was because of them that their children's lives were spoiled. Additionally, the woman prisoner in the study said that the media took photographs of their children and published them in the newspapers. She said that it was already very difficult for them to live without us and the media went a step too far publishing photographs of their children.

Some prisoners' families lived in the city where the prison was located. I visited three such homes which were in close proximity to the prison. The families lived in abject poverty. They earned Rs. 150/- (3 Euros approximately) as daily wages. The wife of the prisoner told me that if they did not work for a day they would go hungry that particular day. During the home visit the prisoner's sons asked me, 'When is our father going to be released?' These children did not have a photograph of their father and did not know for a long time what he looked like because they were two and four years old when he was arrested. Hence the prisoner asked one of his fellow prisoners to draw a portrait of him so that he could send it to his sons.

One of the greatest disappointments for both the prisoner and the partner was when children blamed them for the incarceration and the crime. A prisoner's wife told her children that their father was innocent but when the children grew up, they questioned their father's innocence. The wife said that, 'When they were children, I begged on the streets for money to keep them alive and now when they question their father's innocence my heart breaks'.

The Process of Death Penalty

The process of death penalty has emerged from the narration of the prisoners about their experiences and perceptions from their arrest till they were sentenced to death. The data revealed seven processes that a prisoner had to go through while being sentenced to death. It begins with their arrest, being in the lock-up, appearance before the magistrate for the first time, either sent back to lock-up or sent to judicial custody (prison), being in judicial custody, trial and being sentenced to death. In this process, prisoners meet various actors such as media personnel, doctors, lawyers, magistrates, judges, police, prison officers, prison visitors and family members. These actors play a significant role in the process of prisoners being sentenced to death. While these actors play a role in the sentencing of prisoners, they do not necessarily stick to one process but were woven into the process of being sentenced to death.

Process 1: Arrest

An arrest is defined as depriving a person of liberty by legal authority; in the technical criminal law sense, to seize an alleged or suspected offender to answer for a crime.[12] The study encapsulates the confrontation with criminal justice system beginning with the arrest thus making it the first process of death penalty. Arrest of a person highlights three characteristics, namely 'class and/or caste', 'coerced' and 'charged'.

Prisoners are poor, marginalised and socially excluded.[13] Education is an indicator of their class and caste. Among the 111 prisoners interviewed, 17 per cent were complete illiterates and 53 per cent were educated up to the tenth grade. This indicated the low level of education which pushes them to take up menial jobs which do not provide adequate income to sustain a family. Thus most of the prisoners (70 per cent) were daily wage workers or casual labourers who earned Rs. 120/- (2 Euros) or less per day. Around 15 per cent of prisoners were also unemployed when they were arrested. Hence it proves that most of these prisoners came from socially and economically poor backgrounds. Of these prisoners 41 per cent of the prisoners belonged to lower caste or ethnic minority. People from the lower castes often are trapped in the circle of poverty because of their social and spatial exclusion. Prisoners themselves said that they were arrested because they belonged to an oppressed class or caste. Furthermore, prisoners from religious minority claimed that they were arrested because of their religion. In caste violence where prisoners were arrested, they

12 Gifis, Steven H. *Barron's Law Dictionary*. Hauppauge, NY: Barron's Educational Series, Inc., 2010.

13 Wacquant. 'Deadly symbiosis when ghetto and prison meet and mesh'.

claimed that in spite of the fact that there was an entire mob attacking the victims; they were arrested because of their caste identity. However, almost 50 per cent of the prisoners refused to disclose their caste identity.

Further prisoners said that they were 'coerced' into being arrested. In most cases, prisoners reported that they were taken to a police station with an assurance that they would be sent home immediately. However, in reality, they were never let out even on bail and finally were awarded the death sentence. For instance, one prisoner who was arrested in the evening was told, 'We will do an enquiry and send you in the morning'. In another case, the prisoner said that he was with his family and at 7:30 a.m. a guard came and told him that the Circle Inspector has summoned him to the police station regarding a case. The guard also informed him that there was no complaint lodged or a First Report Information (FIR) reported. So this prisoner went to the police station alone and he was taken to a different district. He said that he was kept in the lock-up for 17 days without being produced in the court even once.

Prisoners also reported that it was a common practice to arrest the family members along with the so called 'main or prime' accused. Thus a lot of auxiliary arrests took place. In some cases, the family members were released but in most cases where family members were arrested, they spend time on death row together. According to the prisoners, this was a tactic by the police to get the 'main' accused 'confess' the crime. Once the accused signed a 'confessional statement', the family members were released. When family members were arrested, they were either arrested from their homes or at times when they came to visit the prisoner in judicial custody (prison). According to the prisoners, it was the prison officials who informed the police about these visits thus revealing the nexus between them. It was most evident in the recent Arun Ferreira case where he was abducted outside the prison in front of his family members by the police for another case. The family saw him being taken away in a van by persons in civil clothes. The police knew the date and time of his release through the prison officials.[14]

In a similar case of nexus between police and prison officials in the process of arrest, a particular prisoner who was accused of 45 murders had a visit from his wife. This prisoner told his wife, 'My grandfather said, whenever we are in trouble go to Indira Gandhi (ex-Prime Minister of India) and now that she is no more please go and meet Sonia Gandhi (Daughter-in-law). She will definitely help us.' This woman set out for the capital city – Delhi – to meet Sonia Gandhi. According to this prisoner, she could not meet Sonia Gandhi but

14 Maitra, Pradeep Kumar. 'After four years, 'Naxalite' Arun Ferreira walks free'. *Hindustan Times*, Nagpur, 4 January 2012. See http://www.hindustantimes.com/india-news/after-four-years-naxalite-arun-ferreira-walks-free/article1-791172.aspx (last accessed 27 March 2015).

she met Margaret Alwa, the then head of The Ministry of Women and Child Welfare. The wife told Margaret Alwa that if they do not stop the injustice, she and her children will commit suicide. According to him Margaret Alwa assured his wife that they would look into the matter. He said that since the government had given an assurance that they will look into the matter, the wife came back. As promised, this minister issued a letter to the state enquiring about the case. The next time when the prisoner's wife came to the prison to meet him; she was arrested in the meeting room. It was the prison officials who informed the police. The prisoner said that he felt helpless watching her being arrested because of him. He did not know about her custody for a long time and had to fight with the magistrate to know the whereabouts of his wife.

Another aspect of 'coercion' in the process of arrest was that even though the prisoners were arrested by 'force', the police recorded it as 'surrendered'. A prisoner said that when the crime occurred he was not in his village but he saw his photograph in the daily newspaper. He was afraid to go back to his village yet he went back and when he was there, he was immediately arrested.

When a person is arrested, they are charged with a certain crime on the basis of the Indian Penal Code, 1860. But prisoners reported that they were arrested for a certain crime but charged with some 'bigger' crime. Many prisoners reported that they were involved in petty crimes such as theft earlier, but they clearly were not involved in the crime they were charged for. For instance, one prisoner said, 'Madam, we had a criminal record earlier for theft or dacoity. However, when there was an unsolved murder in a particular jurisdiction we were arrested and charged for those unsolved murders'. These were typical cases where a whole family (large clan) was arrested and everyone was charged with murder and dacoity. This happened in two states where the similarity between the families and the kind of crime they were awarded death sentence for were very similar. Both families belonged to lower castes, they had no capacity to hire lawyers, they were both charged with murder and dacoity, and in both cases there were two or three juveniles arrested and the awarded death penalty. Family one reported that a young boy from the family stole a silver article from a house. In order to get 'rid' of it they sold it. However the shop owner informed the police and the whole family of 9–10 members were arrested. They were later shown as a big gang and all the murder cases which were 'unsolved' in that jurisdiction were charged on this family. In family two six were arrested and had similar charges raised against them. All of them claimed to be innocent and even said that they had their names registered in a daily wage register where they were working when the said crime occurred. One of them who claimed to be innocent said, 'I can lie to you but lying to my own conscience will only kill me. I want my case to be re-opened'. But they did not have any support to prove their innocence and thus serve their time on death row, waiting to be executed. Similarly another prisoner said that he was involved in *ganja* (drug) cases earlier but he was charged with murder.

Many prisoners claimed to be juveniles when they were arrested. According to Indian Law, no juvenile can be arrested and tried in a normal court.[15] They have to be tried in a juvenile court and a juvenile cannot be on death row according to this law. I have asked many younger-looking prisoners their age when they were arrested. Many of them said they were below the age of 18. Two of the prisoners on death row who participated in the study were released from the prison after 10 years and three years in prison. There are still many prisoners on death row who were juveniles when the crime was committed.

The return of Lombroso-style mythologies about criminal atavism and the wide diffusion of bestial metaphors in the journalistic and political field (where mention of 'superpredators', 'wolf-packs', 'animals' and the like are commonplace), the massive over-incarceration of blacks has supplied a powerful common-sense warrant for 'using colour as a proxy for dangerousness'.[16] In the Indian context, it is not a 'return' but a 'style' that existed for a long time since 1871 when the British Raj introduced the 'Criminal Tribes Act, 1871' where once a tribe became 'notified' as criminal, all its members were required to register with the local magistrate, failing which they would be charged with a crime under the Indian Penal Code, 1860. Though this act was repealed in 1952 with the Habitual Offenders Act, 1952, certain tribes and people are still registered with the police authorities as 'habitual offenders'. They also claim that people from this 'list' are still picked up in case of any offence in a particular jurisdiction. I confirm this because as a social worker in the women's prison, women prisoners who were termed 'habitual offenders' were the ones to be picked up first when there was a reported crime. For instance, when there is a First Information Report lodged for a stolen phone in a particular jurisdiction, then the first persons to be picked up are the 'habitual offenders'.

Process 2: Being in the Lock-up

Strictly speaking, the word 'prisoner' includes persons confined in both police and prison custody. A cell inside a police station, or a secured and guarded room attached to it, is usually referred to as the 'lock-up'. Persons detained on suspicion, or arrested, are kept by the police for the purpose of interrogation.[17] Thus the second process is 'being in the lock-up' or any place where a prisoner

15 Juvenile Justice (Care and Protection of Children) Act, 2000.

16 Kennedy, Randall. 'Race, law and suspicion: Using color as a proxy for dangerousness', in *Race, Crime and the Law*. New York: Pantheon, 1997, pp. 136–67; cited in Wacquant, Loïc. 'The new "peculiar institution": On the prison as surrogate ghetto'. *Theoretical Criminology* 4, no. 3 (2000): 377–89.

17 Tata Institute of Social Sciences. *Forced Separation: Children of Imprisoned Mothers (An Exploration in Two Indian Cities)*. Mumbai: Prayas Publications, 2002.

is detained or confined. This is a process that burdens the prisoners both physically and emotionally and is described the most in the interview. Many of the prisoners were taken to lodges, bungalows, secluded construction sites or empty houses. All these places served a 'perfect atmosphere' to intimidate, torture or extract confessions from prisoners. Prisoners who were 'confined' in these different locations were not produced before the magistrates within 24 hours of arrest as the law prescribes. Prisoners reported that they were produced after 45 or 22 or 17 or 14 days of confinement. For instance, one prisoner said that two of them were arrested together and housed in a particular police station for 15 days. Thereafter they were taken to a new building and were 'confined' in this new building for over three and a half months. Another one said, 'I was arrested on so and so date from my house. I was first taken to a police station but later to a lodge and from there to a bungalow'. This prisoner even remembered the name and room number of the lodge where he was taken.

When prisoners were confined in places other than a police lock-up, their family members were not informed of this. Even when the family members enquired with the police, they were not given any information. In one particular case, the prisoner told how his father ran from pillar to post to enquire about him. He said that his father went to the Tehesil (district) office to lodge a complaint but the Tehesildar (district collector) did not file the complaint and drove him away. He said that if the District Collector would have enquired, the police would have been forced to produce him in court the next day. He said that his father also went to the police station with a written complaint that the son was missing but the officers refused to take this complaint.

I remember a joke that was shared widely, when I was growing up. I found the joke very funny and always shared it. Now I call it morbid humour. The United Kingdom, Russia and India were given the task of investigating a murder. The United Kingdom started an investigation and arrested the accused in one day; Russia took three days and also found and arrested the accused. The Indian police seemed to vanish for a month and finally they were found in a jungle with a monkey tied to the tree; hitting it and telling it, 'Confess that you have done it, tell how you did it?'

The most widely accepted definition of torture is the one used in the United Nations Convention against Torture and Other Cruel, Inhuman or Degrading Treatment or Punishment, 1987 which defines torture as:

> Any act by which severe pain, whether physical or mental, is intentionally inflicted on a person for such purposes as obtaining from him or a third person, information or a confession, punishing him for an act he or a third person has committed or is suspected of having committed, or intimidating or coercing him or a third person, or for any reason based on discrimination of any kind, when such pain or suffering is inflicted by or at the instigation of or with the

> consent or acquiescence of a public official or other person acting in an official capacity. It does not include pain or suffering arising only from, inherent in or incidental to lawful sanctions.

The primary reason for torture was to extract 'confessions' from a person. Indian law is very clear that confessions made to a police officer are not admissible as evidence. However, this same law mentions that if confessions lead to the finding of corroborating evidence then those confessions are still of use to police.[18] So if a crime is 'solved' on the basis of the illegal extraction of evidence, that evidence is still admissible. Similarly another law prohibits the use of a statement of an accused recorded by a police officer and prohibits the police officer from obtaining the signature of a person on the statement made by the accused.[19] Despite this, it was common practice for the police to force detainees to sign statements or blank sheets of paper. Nevertheless there are loopholes in the law. Some laws termed as black laws or draconian laws are used in terrorism-related cases.[20] In these laws, a confession is admissible in the court, if an executive magistrate or a senior ranking police officer is present.

The term 'torture' was used in the context of any physical, verbal, sexual and mental abuse the prisoners faced in police custody. While some prisoners chose to be brief about torture saying, 'It is very common for people to be slapped while arrested and it is very common for officers to abuse and swear at us'; others described their experiences in precise detail, even to the extent of documenting it and handing over the narration to me in written format. A criticism often levelled at the penitentiary system in the early nineteenth century was that a condemned individual should suffer physically more than other individuals. Thus there remained a trace of torture in the modern mechanisms of criminal justice.[21] Prisoners on death row talked about this 'trace' of torture that they faced when they lost their liberty.

Narratives surrounding torture in lock-up were not only about the creation of shame, fear and extreme pain but also a part of the general discourse of torture that contributes to the fact that body was used as a means to exercise power. It was the shame of being tortured that lingered in the minds of these prisoners. The body is also directly involved in a political field; power relations have an immediate hold upon it; they invest it, mark it, train it, torture it, force

---

18 Indian Evidence Act, 1872 (Sections 25, 26, 27).

19 The Code of Criminal Procedure,1973 (Section 162).

20 Prevention of Terrorism Act of India, 2002; Terrorist and Disruptive Activities (Prevention) Act of India, 1993; Karnataka Control of Organised Crime Act, 2000; Maharashtra Control of Organised Crime Act, 1999.

21 Foucault, Michel. *Discipline and Punish: The Birth of the Prison.* New York: Vintage, 1977.

it to carry out tasks, to perform ceremonies, to emit signs. It must reproduce it in ceremonies that apply to the body of the guilty person in the form of humiliation and pain.[22] In India we still reproduce the 'ceremonies' that apply to the body of the guilty person in the form of shaming, humiliation and pain but inducing fear by threatening and tutoring. Prisoners accounted their experiences with great pain where most of them broke down. When prisoners were first brought into custody, they lost their orientation about the place they were taken to. It is not uncommon that this happens.[23]

All the prisoners who described torture echoed one statement – 'I have no idea how I survived that pain'. In custody, according to the prisoners, it always began with terrorising and intimidating the accused which broke them down. A large number of prisoners said, 'They did regular work' in police custody. It took a while for me to comprehend that 'regular work' meant torture. Prisoners described various types of torture such as 'Bombay cut', third degree torture and *maar-peet* (hitting). When an officer does a 'Bombay cut' on the prisoner it means that one is asked to sit on a chair, a rod is placed under the knee, hands are tied behind the back joining the thumb with a cloth and one is hit on the back. Another kind of 'Bombay cut' was when one's hands are tied back joining the thumb with a piece of cloth, one is pulled up with another cloth to a hook on the ceiling thus suspending the body in the air and hitting on the feet. Another prisoner said that hands were tied with a rope and he was suspended in the air and he was hit with the butt of the gun. Yet another prisoner said that he was suspended to a fan and was hit on the toe; the toe nails came off. He could not eat properly for ten days because of the pain. Later a tablet was administered to him following which he did not remember anything and said 'yes' to everything the police asked for.

Prisoners reported of lower back pain, while some showed me marks on their knees, some showed me broken teeth. The day I visited a certain prison, a prisoner was eating bread dipped in milk because he was unable to open his mouth. He said that when he was in the lock-up his mouth was shut with a clip and therefore he could not open his jaws properly even years later.

When prisoners described torture as 'regular work' one of them said that he was hit with a belt because of which his tooth fell off. He said that the police hit them with a belt which leaves no marks on the body. Another prisoner was asked to kneel and a big rod was rolled on his thighs. His ankles were twisted and one officer stood on his feet with his boots. Many prisoners said that they were chained in their cells while in police lock-up. This sometimes stretched over a month. One of the prisoners said that his legs were pierced with sharp

---

22 Ibid.

23 Benvenisti, Meron. *Abu Ghraib: The Politics of Torture.* Berkeley, CA: North Atlantic Books, 2004.

nails and that it took three months to heal and during this time he could not walk without limping or turn properly while sleeping. He said that he had lost count of how many times his feet were pierced with sharp nails by a certain police officer.

Torture is often calculated, organised, technically thought out. It may be subtle, may neither make use of weapons nor of terror, yet remain of a physical type.[24] This kind of torture indeed used 'instruments' but it was subtle and did not show any external injuries. For instance, a prisoner was made to eat large quantities of salt- as much as a whole cup. In addition to this his urethra was blocked with a stick and this prisoner had to undergo this 'treatment' thrice a day and 'all he had to do' was to 'accept' that he committed the murder. The police officer told him that if he accepted the murder he will be released immediately. Another form of torture which did not leave any injuries was when a ball pen was inserted between nails and skin and then hammered and lemon juice was squeezed on it. Many reported that another method of inducing pain without marks was electrocuting the prisoner. The prisoners called it 'current'. The most common method in this strategy was to place a clip on the ears, lips, nipples and penis and administer electric current. A similar way of inducing pain without marks was when a prisoner was stripped and pushed into a five feet tub filled with water and ice blocks. There were four fans in the corners and he was made to stand there from 8:30 p.m. to 5:45 a.m. Another prisoner told how he was given electric shock and was drowned in water. When he went for a medical check-up, the doctor gave a 'normal' certificate. Some prisoners were not only electrocuted but also poked with rods in their knees. I could see the injury marks on his knees even on the day of the interview. One of the prisoners said that his head tore open because he was hit with a rod. He was taken under a false name to a private doctor who gave him medicine. He was however, not allowed to talk to anyone. Prisoners came into contact with doctors who were agents outside the field of criminal justice system and yet are fundamental actors to sustain the system. Another prisoner said that he was taken to a Civil Hospital but there were no case papers, he was just given medicines for his wounds.

The next form of torture included causing pain to private parts of the body. Again these were places where injuries cannot be immediately seen. For instance when a prisoner was asked to confess, he was handcuffed and his legs were spread in 'V' shape; a brick was suspended on a string on one end and the other end was tied to his penis while he was on the table. In another case, a rod covered with salt was inserted into a prisoner's anus. They did this to him every half-an-hour and the police officer told him that he must admit that he committed the murder or else they would keep repeating it. Another prisoner was similarly tortured but the police inserted his anus with a rod covered with lemon juice and

24 Foucault. *Discipline and Punish.*

chilli powder. He said that he passed blood in his stools for several days after this incident. One of the prisoners said that when he asked for water, the police officer urinated on him and said 'Drink this'. This prisoner said that when he was really very thirsty he drank his own urine to survive. Another prisoner said that the police applied chilli powder to his private parts after removing his pubic hair one by one and this prisoner said that he could not stand up on his own for more than 10–15 minutes. He also said that he still could not sleep because of the incidences of torture which appeared whenever he tried to sleep. One of them said that he was handcuffed, stripped, electrocuted and petrol was poured into his private parts. He said that all of these happened in front of his wife which was very humiliating for him. Another prisoner said that he was given 'current' (electrocuted) in his private parts at regular intervals throughout the day and then the police officer put salt and pepper into his private parts which were again electrocuted. One prisoner said that he was ashamed of telling me, a woman, of the torture that he had to face in custody. However he still recounted and said that he was stripped in the lock-up and petrol was poured in his anus and all over his body and he was beaten up the whole night. He was asked to sign blank papers and confess his crime. He said that for over three months he could not walk because of the torture and when he thinks about the torture in police custody his heart sinks and 'skips a beat'. He also said that this incident was just an ounce of what he actually had to face in custody.

Prisoners were tortured by means of inducing fear. This was similar to what happened in Abu Ghraib, where dogs were brought in to scare prisoners.[25] In one instance, a prisoner said that he was stripped down, handcuffed, both his legs were spread and two snakes were left in the cell. The prisoner said that when the snake came near him, he was scared and completely terrified. The police first dropped in a small snake and then a bigger one. He said that both the snakes crawled towards him and one even bit him and he thought that he would die soon. He said that he was left with the snakes for almost three hours. Another prisoner was told that he should confess his crime because no one knew of his arrest. Therefore they threatened to kill him and dispose his body in the forest and say that he was murdered by one of his enemies because he was in the real estate business. This prisoner was afraid that he would be killed and hence confessed to the 'crime' out of fear. In some instance, the police used strategies such as, 'Your brother has accepted the crime, what is your problem? Just sign the paper'.

Another prisoner was threatened with being tied up in a gunny bag and placed on the railway track. He reasoned with himself that he would confess to the crime instead of dying this way. He said that he had committed just

25 Luban, David. 'Human dignity, humiliation and torture'. *Kennedy Institute of Ethics Journal* 19, no. 3 (2009): 211–30.

one theft but would rather say that he had committed 50 more thefts and take the punishment than die in a gruesome manner. He ultimately confessed and signed the blank sheet. The Attica Rebellion in 1971 began when prisoners demanded better living conditions in the prison but another triggering factor of the rebellion was the fact that Jackson David was killed in custody while he was 'trying to escape' prison. No black leader believes that it is true.[26] The United States and India are not much different when it comes to the exercising of power. One of the prisoner's accounts reminded me of Jackson David because the officer told him, 'We will take you outside the jail road and shoot you down. We'll say that you were trying to escape the prison'. Another one was threatened that if he did not confess his crime, they would kill him and throw his body into a lake and no one would know about it.

Yet another prisoner was arrested for his alleged connection with a dacoit along with 10–12 other people. He said that this dacoit attacked a police jeep and killed six police officers. That same day, police officers came, randomly blindfolded a few persons who were held in the bungalow with him, took them to the forest and shot them. The second time the police came and took six more members from among the people and shot them too. He said that the police guard informed him about this incident and told him that he was 'lucky' that he was not picked up. He said that he was in fear for his life and prayed that he should soon be taken to jail. His explanation of this random shooting of people (taken from detention) was that when the dacoit attacked the police van, the police also wanted to show the outside world that they too killed the dacoit's men in an encounter. Another prisoner who was allegedly a 'terrorist' said that he was given no sleep, no clothes and terrorised and intimidated by the police. The police wanted to know the other 'terror plans in India' that he knew of.

In another instance, the inspector took a prisoner to the spot where the crime had occurred. Then the police showed him pictures and told them, 'You have to tell that this is where you entered from and this is how you committed the crime'. The next day the police officer took this prisoner to the same place along with a journalist. They made a video of this and he was asked to repeat the tutored part of 'how he did the crime'. Prisoners also said that their photos were published in the newspaper which did not help them. These photographs were given to the media by the police. One of the prisoners said that the police and the media were hand-in-glove and the police tell the journalist that they will give them 'juicy' crime stories for their reports but in return should turn a blind eye to the torture happening in custody.

The only woman who participated in this study told me that the police took her to a rented house. The officer told her that she has to do whatever they said. She further said that the police electrocuted her and put chilli powder

26 Davis, Angela Y. *Are Prisons Obsolete?*. New York: Seven Stories Press, 2003.

in her vagina. She was stripped naked in front of her male relatives. This was very humiliating and shameful for her. She was also threatened with rape. Her husband was also in the same detention place and told her to accept whatever the police asked her. Another prisoner talked about his wife who was arrested but later released. He said that she was five months pregnant with their second child. She was given electric shock on her breast, ears and fingers in front of him and she had to be hospitalised for three to four months after she was released.

Another prisoner who was arrested for rape and murder said that one day, in custody, he was given faeces to eat. He said he was kept naked all the time in the police lock-up and one night around five to six women came to the police station at night. He realised that they were *vaishayas* (sex workers). He said that the officer present there pulled his penis so hard that it started bleeding and told him 'Now come on, rape these women'. Later he was also dressed up as a woman. Another prisoner who said that the police did 'regular work' on him but what was shameful and humiliating was when his family was 'called' to the police station to watch it. He was made to lie down, a big log was rolled on his thighs, chilli powder was put on his penis and eyes. The police officer said that if he did not accept the crime, they would 'work' on him again and rape his mother and wife. He said that he was completely naked in front of them and that all of them cried and he accepted all the crime he was asked to confess to. Similarly, another prisoner said that his parents were arrested with him. The police put a rod into his anus and asked him to sign blank papers in front of his parents. He was given food twice a day and he said that 'When they gave me food, I knew they will hit me'. He eventually signed all the blank papers he was asked to. The only reason the police officers stopped beating the prisoners was when another officer told them that the prisoner might die in custody and that would be a 'bigger headache'.

Lombroso may have been the most prominent practitioner applying Social Darwinism to criminality. He concluded that about 40 per cent of criminals followed hereditary compulsion; others acted from passion, rage, or desperation.[27] Lombroso even though criticised heavily for making this connection of certain facial features and criminal tendencies; the police used that to their advantage. A police officer told a prisoner, 'Sign the confessional statement. I know you have murdered because we have learned in our training session that criminals have facial features like yours'. The prisoner said that he felt humiliated to hear that he 'looked' like a criminal or murderer to the police officer.

There are actors and directors while performing theatre, likewise, the present death row prisoners, the then accused, were actors and they were 'tutored' to

27 Gould, Stephen Jay. *The Mismeasure of Man*. New York: Norton, 1996; cited in Freitag, Sandria B. 'Crime in the social order of colonial north India'. *Modern Asian Studies* 25, no. 2 (1991): 227–61.

'deliver' dialogues which were scripted by the police officers.[28] The medium used for this 'performance' was by means of threatening and tutoring the accused. Further, the use of language in this phenomenon caused fear and pain. Consequently, these phenomena form the very politics of being in custody which leads to the death penalty. The 'self-evident' characteristic of prisons is based on 'deprivation of liberty'.[29] Nevertheless, the process of 'deprivation of liberty' begins with arrest and continues in the lock-up and only then does it further percolate to the prison.

One of the prisoners arrested in a terrorism-related case said that he was not physically tortured, but he was mentally harassed at every moment he was in the Central Bureau of Investigation custody. The officers interrogated him 24–7 and he was not allowed to sleep. He said that, 'The Indian government like the Bush Administration would dismiss this kind of mental torture calling it an "enhanced interrogation technique"'. At one point, he was so fed up with the continuous interrogation that he was ready to sign anything and everything they asked him to. The officers wrote a confessional statement and asked him to sign it. The latter told them that he was literate and insisted on reading it. They were very reluctant to give him the statement but they eventually gave it to him. He made some changes in that statement and after that an officer came with a new copy and asked him to sign it. This time he was forced to sign it without reading the new copy and said that he was not sure what changes they had made in that copy. Only 13 per cent of the prisoners were arrested for terrorism-related crimes which meant that their confessions in front of a senior ranking officer could be taken as evidence. The remaining 87 per cent of the prisoners were arrested in crimes where a confessional statement obtained in custody would not be admissible in a court of law. However all prisoners were asked to sign blank documents and were tortured in custody to 'extract' this confession.

All of them said that it was better to die than to go through this kind of torture. When they were asked to sign the blank sheets for confession, they reasoned with themselves 'Why should I die here? Let me just sign whatever they ask me to. At least I will have my life'. When asked if these incidents were reported, all the prisoners echoed in the same voice that it was futile to raise any complaint. The ones who complained said that action against torture only existed on paper and that in reality nothing happened. Many prisoners wrote letters to the Ministers of Law and Justice and also to both the State and National Human Rights Commissions. They showed me copies of their complaints and petitions. None of them received any replies.

---

28 Schechner, Richard and Mady Schuman, eds. *Ritual, Play and Performance: Readings in the Social Sciences/Theatre*. New York: Seabury Press, 1976.

29 Foucault. *Discipline and Punish*.

The longest time a prisoner spent in prison was 22 years while the shortest was three years. Nevertheless when they narrated about the torture they had to go through in custody it as if it happened yesterday. Most of them said that they still have pain in various parts of their bodies because of the torture. One of the prisoners said that on most of the days, he woke up in the middle of the night and yelled 'Please do not hit me'.

Process 3: Appearing before the Magistrate and other Actors for the First Time

The next stage after the arrest and the police lock-up is 'being taken before the magistrate for the first time' which according to the Criminal Procedure Code, 1973 should be within 24 hours of the arrest. Before being taken to the magistrate, the prisoners are tutored to say that they were not harmed while they were in custody. The magistrates while questioning the prisoner if s/he was tortured in custody gives a mere lip-service to the D.K. Basu guideline.[30] These guidelines, a judgment by Supreme Court issued certain requirements to be followed as preventive measures against custodial violence in all cases of arrest or detention 'till legal provisions are made in that behalf'. Magistrates did not verify about being hit in custody, prisoners were not sent to judicial custody (prison) even when they complained of tortured in custody. These are some of the instances where magistrates have to take action according to the D.K. Basu guidelines. The prisoners gave a different reality when appearing before the court.

A large number of prisoners were taken to the magistrate's house at night. According to the prisoners, this made easy for the police to get the prisoner back into custody and also to hide marks on the body as they were less visible at night. This was also the process where they were tutored to say things. No matter when the prisoner was arrested, s/he was tutored to say that s/he was arrested a day before. Also the police officer 'tutored' prisoners telling them '*Magistrate ke saamne kuch nahi bolneka*' (do not say anything in front of the magistrate). They were then threatened that if they spoke before the magistrate, the police officials would repeat the 'regular work' when they were returned to custody. In one instance, a prisoner did not follow this 'tutoring' instead he removed his clothes and showed his injuries to the magistrate. However, the magistrate did not make a note of it and sent him back to police custody for another 15 days. He was beaten even more for 'telling' the magistrate when he was 'tutored' not to.

In addition to that, the use of language also played a very important role in the threatening-tutoring phenomenon. The police officers used the word, 'work' instead of torture. For example, before taking to the magistrate, police

30 D. K. Basu v State of West Bengal – AIR (SC)-610, 1997-SCC-1-416.

officers told the prisoner, 'Do not tell anything to the magistrate or we will further "work" on you. If the magistrate asks you "How did this happen?" (His legs were blue with all the beatings in custody), you have to say that "the public beat you outside"'. In the court this prisoner said exactly as he was asked to because he was scared that he would be beaten again. Prisoners were coerced to speak in front of the magistrate to fit the 'police version' of the arrest. One of the prisoners was asked to tell that he was arrested in a particular state and not the other state where he was originally arrested.

The prisoners confirm the fact that each police officer knew exactly which magistrate would ask what question. The accused were tutored accordingly before they were taken to the magistrate. The officer tutored this prisoner that the magistrate would ask '*Taklif diya kya?*' (Were you given trouble?). The officer tutored him to say '*nahi diya' bolna*' (Say you were not given any trouble). This was exactly what the magistrate asked and he responded like he was tutored. Threatening-tutoring also worked in cases where the prisoners' family members were in danger. The police told this particular prisoner that if he did not say exactly what they told him, they would burn his parents' house down. He said that when he went to court, he just signed the file and did not open his mouth because he was scared for his parents' lives.

The only woman prisoner was also tutored before she was taken to the magistrate. She informed me that she was in an illegal detention for three months before being taken to court. The police officer told her that she should not mention the three months in detention but should say that she was arrested two days ago. They threatened her that if she did not say what she was told to, that she would be taken back to the same detention place and be raped.

A few prisoners reported that they were given sedatives before they were taken to the magistrate. One reported that, 'I was taken to the Deputy Superintendent of Police's office and was given a tablet to eat. This tablet made me drowsy and I could not speak in court'. In another instance, a prisoner said that before he was taken to court, he was given *biryani* (meat cooked with rice), alcohol and *ganja* (weed) which made him drowsy.

According to the prisoners, some magistrates did not ask them anything or, even worse, did not even look at them. A prisoner said, 'I was produced before the magistrate, but he did not look at me or ask me anything, I was sent to a sub-jail immediately'. Talking about the magistrate's indifference towards them, one said, 'When I was arrested, I was remanded for two days. Then I was taken to the magistrate's house. The magistrate was on the roof top. He did not listen to me – he just talked to the police officer and thereafter we were asked to leave'. Another prisoner had a similar account, 'When I was taken to the magistrate, he did not ask me anything and I was given back to police custody for a month'. Another prisoner said that he was badly injured and hospitalised for six months and was deliberately not taken to the magistrate for six months. According to him, if the police had taken him to court, the magistrate would have given him a bail based on his medical condition.

Tutoring not only worked prior to taking them before the magistrates but also before senior police inspectors and media. One reporter asked a prisoner, 'Did you commit the murder?' The prisoner wanted to beg the journalist to rescue him but when he looked at the police officer, the officer signalled him to say 'yes'. This prisoner was forced to admit to the journalist that he had committed the murder. The officer replied on the prisoner's behalf and said, 'Pakka (For sure) he has done it, Madam'.

Process 4: Either sent back to the Lock-up or sent to Judicial Custody

The next process is a transition phase where prisoners were either sent back to lock-up or to judicial custody (prison). If the prisoner was sent back to the lock-up, they had to undergo the same as above. The ones who were sent back to the lock-up were taken before the magistrate after a day or two or after a maximum period of 14 days. After this they were transferred to judicial custody i.e. the prison. However there were certain exceptions in this process as well. In one instance, a prisoner reported that he was held in police custody for 'enquiry' for a period of 30 days.

Process 5: Sent to Judicial Custody

The next process leading to the death penalty is being sent to judicial custody or magisterial custody or prison or jail. While continuing to remain in prison during the period of trial, the individual's legal status is that of an 'accused person'. To distinguish this category of prisoners from sentenced prisoners, the term commonly used by the administration is 'undertrial'.[31] Wacquant states that the ones who should not be seen outside in society are the ones sent to the prison.[32] This subsequent process of 'trial' and 'being sentenced to death' happens while prisoners are in judicial custody. They had to follow a certain discipline; they belonged to the category of individuals who have lost their agency.[33]

When an accused is taken from police custody into judicial custody, a health ticket has to be issued. There were two ways of interpreting this health ticket. A prison officer said that it was mainly done when an accused is tortured in the lock-up and has died in prison, then prison officers did not want to be

31 Tata Institute of Social Sciences. *Forced Separation.*

32 Wacquant. 'Deadly symbiosis when ghetto and prison meet and mesh'.

33 Goffman, Erving. 'On the characteristics of total institutions', in Walter Reed Army Institute of Research: *Symposium on preventive and social psychiatry*. Washington, DC: U.S. Government Printing Office, 1957: 43–84.

responsible for the death. Hence this medical check-up was an 'anticipatory bail' for prison officials in case of death due to torture. Contrary to this, a prisoner said that these medical check-ups were just a formality because in reality the prison doctor did not record any injuries sustained from torture. One prisoner however reported that he was thoroughly checked because his co-accused consumed cyanide capsule and died.

Another process that takes place in judicial custody is an 'identification parade'. This is the process where witnesses (cases where there are eye-witnesses) try to identify the accused. The witnesses are brought into judicial custody by the police. Prisoners describe this process as a very humiliating experience – one reason was that the police or prison officials influenced the witnesses. For instance, the police or prison officials ask the witnesses, 'Isn't this the same person that you saw?' In instances where the witnesses say that it was not the same person, the witnesses would be taken to another room and after a while they would say, 'Yes, it is the same person we saw'. Apart from this, witnesses who were present for the identification parade of the accused were also tutored. In many instances, the witnesses said that they did not know the accused, but then they were taken to a separate room and, according to the prisoner, the witnesses were tutored by the police to say that they were the same boys. Another prisoner recounted that the main witness in his case was under pressure to give a false witness as her husband was also arrested. The police threatened her that if she did not give a statement e will also be prosecuted. So she gave a 'false' witness to protect her husband. After her statement her husband was released. During the identification parade, prisoners also reported that they were called various names based on their crime especially the ones who were accused of rape and murder.

Prison officials and their interaction with the prisoners were dynamic and depict power play. Prison officials said that even if the prisoner has committed 100 murders, when they came to the prison they were automatically subdued and intimidated by the prison. One of the prison officers told me that when prisoners come to the prison, they lose half their 'smartness'. A prison officer told me that officially prisoners were 'guests in custody' and prison officials were the custodians. One of the prison officers said, 'We are the custodians of prisoners. We treat them well, we feed them. What more does one want?' However the prisoners perceived that the prison officers did not act in the interest of the prisoners; instead they supported the police officers in 'handling' the prisoner.

Many reported that they were beaten by prison officers when they came to judicial custody. While beating one of the prisoners who had been arrested for murder, the prison officer said, 'You have a big body. Why do you have to come to the prison? Why did you make this mistake?' In another case of caste violence, the prison officer who belonged to the same caste as the victim beat the accused who belonged to a different caste and said, 'How dare you kill a person belonging to my caste? We will make sure that you get the harshest punishments even death penalty'. Prisoners who were Muslims and were arrested for terrorism-related crimes recounted experiences of how they felt discriminated against because of their religious identity. One of them said that when he was an undertrial, the Superintendent of the prison was so angry with them (him and his co-accused) that the officer burned their 'Holy Koran' (Holy Scriptures of the Muslims). Besides this, the Muslim prisoners narrated that whenever they asked for an Urdu newspaper, they were called *Pakistanis*. In another case where a certain prisoner whose mother tongue was Urdu wrote letters to the families in Urdu, the letters were not sent. Prisoners called this a violation of their right to be in contact with their family. All letters sent and received in prison are scrutinised for security reasons. Prisoners say that the prison authorities can make a 'trusted' prisoner who can read Urdu read the letter for the system. But prison authorities simply refused to allow the prisoners send or receive letters in Urdu. Prisoners also said that the concept of 'innocent till proven guilty' only exists in legal documents and texts. This was clear in their interactions with prison officials, media personnel and prison visitors.

Most of the prisoners who were on death row were involved in cases which were already hyped in the media. A lot of them were thus already considered 'dangerous' even in prison and were placed in maximum security prison even as an undertrial. Hence there was not much interaction with co-prisoners. In addition to this, there was also a very peculiar process while they were in judicial custody called 'body warrant'. Prisoners reported that the court issues a 'body warrant' against them and thus they were taken out of judicial custody, once again to the lock-up. This makes their situation vulnerable. This is done in order to 'investigate' the crime; however the ones against whom the body warrant is issued becomes vulnerable to torture.

Another set of actors that prisoners interact with while in custody were the prison visitors. In India, prisons are a state subject. The prison visiting system in all Indian states has two types of visitors – The Official Visitors and the Non-official Visitors. The official visitors include the Inspector General of Prisons, the Director of Health Services, the District and Sessions Judge, the Additional District and Sessions Judge, the District Magistrate, the Deputy Inspector General of Police, the Additional District Magistrate, the Sub Divisional Magistrate and the Civil Surgeon or Medical Officer. Non-official Visitors include members of civil society or members of human rights commissions.[34] One of the prisoners said that the State Human Rights Commission's President

34 Jain, Neha and Sreekumar, R. *Behind Bars: A Closer Look at the Prison Visiting System*, The Commonwealth Human Rights Initiative, Madhya Pradesh, 2000. See http://www.humanrightsinitiative.org/publications/prisons/prison_visiting_system.pdf (last accessed 31 July 2015).

who was a retired judge came and said, 'I can only listen to you but do not have any powers to change anything'.

Another prisoner who was arrested for rape and murder recounted that the prison visitor who was an Executive Magistrate asked him, 'Mr. Z tum hai? (Are you Mr. Z?) How many more people have you murdered? How many more rapes have you committed?' This prisoner said that at least five magistrates have asked him questions like these. He blames it on the media which portrayed him as a beast. Another prisoner said that they sometimes do not know who visits them. One of the prisoners who belonged to a case where the trial was delayed for four years complained to the prison visitor about the delay. The visitor asked him regarding the development of the case. When he heard that the cross-examination was going on he told the prisoner, 'Oh in four years, 66 witnesses were examined, it is a great thing. So be happy and don't complain'.

There was an account of an 'unofficial' visitor too. A high ranking police officer came to the prison and interrogated a prisoner who was arrested for kidnapping and murder. The officer asked the prisoner if the victim he had kidnapped was still alive. This prisoner said that if the officer brought up the dignity of his sister who was molested in police custody or the days his elderly mother spent in police lock-up or rescind the false charges brought against his brother who was arrested along with him, or bring back the accused whom the police killed in an encounter; then he would tell the officer if the victim was alive or dead.

There was one positive account of judicial custody from a prisoner who said that judicial custody was not as intimidating as the police lock-up. This prisoner said, 'If we knew that judicial custody is not like police custody, we would not have 'confessed' to our crimes by signing the blank sheets that the police asked us to'. At the same time, he said that there was no assurance that one would not be sent back to the same police against whom one complained.

Process 6: Trial

The next process leading to death penalty is 'trial' which sometimes took over seven years and sometimes two. Prisoners told of their interplay with various actors such as lawyers, public prosecutors, media personnel, magistrates or judges and police. A charge-sheet must be filed within 90 days of arrest.[35] Once the charge-sheet is filed, the case is committed to a Sessions Court or Lower Court or District Court and the trial begins. A court date typically occurs after every 14 days. When the prisoners were taken to the court, they were taken by police who are called escorts. A police van arrives in front of the prison and all prisoners appearing at a particular court are taken together. This could also

35 The Code of Criminal Procedure, 1973 (Section167 (2)(a)(ii)).

mean 50 prisoners a day. The hearing of each case takes place in different court rooms although in the same location. Hence the police escorts wait for all the prisoners to finish their hearing before they are taken back to the prison. Lunch is distributed in the prison at 10 a.m. and dinner at 3 p.m.; which also means that prisoners remain hungry for the whole day. If a fellow prisoner takes food for the prisoner in their absence, then the prisoner gets to eat food; however this is not always the case. Families of prisoners also bring food to the court but according to the prisoners, they have to pay bribes to the escorts for this food to be provided to the prisoner. There was a recent judgment in Maharashtra which said that prisoners have to be provided with dry food if they were in the court the whole day.[36]

In another case, a prisoner told how after he was transferred to the judicial custody he was not taken to court for the next four months because he was a 'terrorist' and according to the state, special escorts or police personnel were needed to take him to court. Even though prisoners have their trial dates every 14 days, prisoners reported that they were not taken to court regularly. One of the reasons for not being taken to court was a lack of police escorts. Escorts were absent due to '*bandobast*' or '*nakabandi*'. *Bandobast* literally means 'preparation' which is providing security and preparing the ground for a politician. *Nakabandi* literally means 'stopping at the junction'. *Naka* (junction) *bandi* (stop) is conducted at junctions to stop vehicles and check them because the police have received information about criminal activities. The first priority is usually given to *bandobast* or *nakabandi* and since the police system is grossly understaffed, there is no one to escort the undertrials to court. This is also one of the reasons for the prolonged trial period.

Since there were a lot of prisoners taken to court at the same time, the escorts made sure that none of them 'escaped'. The most common way to prevent that was by tying prisoners to each other with a rope or handcuffing them. The law in India prohibits the handcuffing of prisoners and, if handcuffed, only with a court order.[37] One of the prisoners reported that his sister wiped the sweat off his brow and it was difficult for him to climb into the police van with his handcuffs on. Another prisoners said that when he was in the police lock-up, he was chained in his cell the whole day from morning until evening because he was a 'dangerous' prisoner according to the police. Prisoners perceived that cattle were treated with much more dignity than them in this situation.

Prisoners used their bodies as a means to protest or show dissent when they have resorted to hunger strikes at various processes after their arrest. In this

---

36 People's Union for Civil Liberties v State of Maharashtra & Anr. Unreported Order dated 30/3/2007 passed by the Bombay High Court in PIL No. 17/2007.

37 Citizen For Democracy Through Its … vs State Of Assam And Others AIR 1996 SC 2193, 1996 CriLJ 3247, (1996) 1 GLR 682.

process, one of the reasons for a hunger strike was if they were not taken to court regularly over a period of time. Another prisoner said that he had to go to 15 different courts. He resorted to hunger striking to get his cases into one court and to have a Central Bureau of Investigation enquiry. All his cases were clubbed together in one court; however, his demand for a Central Bureau of Investigation enquiry did not happen.

During the actual proceedings in a trial, the prisoner talked about their perception and experiences of courts, lawyers, judges and media personnel. The prisoners felt a loss of agency and autonomy in the court rooms. One of them said, 'A Court is like a machine. It could be very well a computer instead of being a human being. No one wants to listen to you'. Court rooms became an institution where prisoners claimed to be 'invisible'. Most of them said that they were not allowed to speak in court and were mostly instructed by their own lawyers. Furthermore, since most of the prisoners on death row were illiterate or did not understand English, it was very difficult for them to understand the court proceedings. At the end of the trial however, prisoners were asked if they had anything to say. One of the prisoners said that there was no point in giving them a chance to speak at the end of the trial as during the whole proceedings they were just 'invisible' and 'mute'.

The prisoners also talked about lawyers – prosecutors and defence lawyers. The prosecutors left no chance to humiliate the prisoners in court. The death penalty in India is given only to the 'rarest of rare' crimes, hence the prosecutor argued in such a manner where s/he proved that it is the 'rarest of rare' crime, that it disturbs the conscience of the society, that the crime was carried out in an extremely brutal, grotesque, diabolical, revolting or dastardly manner. During this process, the prosecutor used various names for the prisoner – devil, blood-thirsty wolf, savage and ruthless person– and argued that the prisoner should not be acquitted or given life imprisonment or he might kill many more. The arguments put forward by the prosecutors were ridiculous according to the prisoners. For instance two prisoners argued their case themselves as they could not afford private lawyers and the government ones were always absent. The prosecutor's argument against the two when demanding the death penalty was, 'When the two of them can actually defend themselves so brilliantly what is the guarantee that they cannot kill?'

Many prisoners reported that one of the 'strategies' where there were more than one accused was to make one accused a pardon-witness. A pardon-witness is a person who is accused of a crime but agrees to be the witness in return for a lesser punishment. A pardon witness has to be produced within 90 days of the arrest, however, in most of the cases, this time period is not observed and a pardon witness is produced even three years into the trial. Prisoners also reported that prosecutors were present when they were interrogated by the police or the Central Bureau of Investigation for the first time. In some cases prosecutors also asked the magistrate to include certain Indian Penal Code sections in the middle of the trial and the magistrates agreed to it. These newly inserted Penal Codes were the ones which fetched them the death sentence.

According to the prisoners, once they sign the '*vakalatnama*' (An authority in writing by litigant to one's lawyer) they give the lawyer the power to determine the fate of their cases. As defence lawyers, most prisoners had legal aid or government lawyers because they could not afford a private lawyer. The legal aid lawyers charged money from the prisoners' families whereas in reality legal aid lawyers are paid by the State. One of the legal aid lawyers asked a prisoner for 10 Lakh Rupees (18,000 Euros approximately) but when the prisoner said that he or the family had no money the lawyer agreed to a sum of Rs. 500/- (9 Euros approximately) per date he appeared. When the family could not bring the money, the lawyer did not appear for the hearing but his assistant came and took another date. Another prisoner narrated how he had to sell his property and his wife's jewellery to pay the lawyer. Many prisoners said that their houses were sold during the trial period to pay the lawyer and their families either lived on the streets or in some relative's houses. One of the prisoners said that his lawyer suggested that he should pay the public prosecutor Five Lakh Rupees (9000 Euros) to dissuade him from arguing in favour of death sentence. This prisoner informed the lawyer that he and his family were very poor and could not raise this huge amount of money. He indeed ended up on death row. There were prisoners who were arrested for dacoity and murder and the prisoners told me, 'Madam if we had really stolen all that money that the police say we had, we could have at least afforded a private lawyer and our families wouldn't be living on the streets'.

Apart from being deliberately absent because of the non-payment of fees, lawyers also went as far as blaming the prisoners for signing blank papers as 'confessional statements' while in custody. One of the lawyers told a prisoner that he should not have signed those blank papers. The prisoner said that instead of arguing in court that the statement was extracted from the prisoner under pressure and intense torture, the lawyer made the prisoner feel guilty about signing the blank paper. Furthermore, in many cases, lawyers were absent during the final arguments and cross-examination. In some instance, when they were present, they cross-examined the witness for ten minutes whereas the prosecutor cross-examined for half an hour. In many cases, the prisoners were alone in the court from the defence side as the lawyers were absent when the judgment for the death sentence was pronounced. Another prisoner said that just before lunch-time, the judge pronounced his sentence in English and left immediately. The prisoner did not understand and the lawyer was absent. The prisoner said that *awaz laganewala* (court-announcer) brought him a judgment copy and asked him to sign it. He was the one who informed the prisoner that he had received *phasisaza* (death sentence).

Another classic behaviour of lawyers according to the prisoners was that most of them did not respond to letters. Furthermore, some lawyers managed to lose crucial documents, such as the proof of their age, which could have eventually secured their release. To top that, they evaded the responsibility of obtaining a duplicate copy of these documents. Contrary to this, some prisoners also reported being satisfied with their legal aid lawyers. One of them said that the lawyer appeared for every hearing. Another prisoner said that the Supreme Court lawyer he had was extremely proactive and replied to the letters that he wrote. In another case, the prisoner said that he was very happy with the lawyer but this lawyer was attacked by the victim's family members and hence could no longer continue with the case. The prisoner had to take a legal aid lawyer because he could not afford to pay another private lawyer a second time.

Another actor in this process is the judge or the magistrate. For most of the prisoners, the judges represented 'authorities' who were on a higher platform both literally and figuratively. In many instances these judges were transferred before they could pronounce the sentence because of routine transfer. According to the prisoners, some cases were influenced by political parties and some judges were deliberately transferred. In one case of transfer, the prisoner narrated that the judge wanted to talk to him alone and the police told her, 'Madam he is a dangerous Muslim fundamentalist'. The judge replied that he might be dangerous for the policeman but not for her and insisted that she wanted to talk to him alone. She enquired about his treatment in police custody. This prisoner said that this incident restored his trust in the judiciary. He was not treated as a 'terrorist' and 'someone to be scared of' just because he had a Muslim name or a beard. In this case, the judge was transferred to another court immediately after this incident. In another case a particular group of prisoners were acquitted in 45 cases due to lack of evidence, therefore according to them, this judge was also transferred. The prisoner said that the next judge who came was 'not good'. This judge gave them the death penalty in almost all the other cases. The lawyer even argued that they had already spent ten years in prison and could be released but the judge went on to give them the death penalty.

Prisoners have also been 'angry' with their judges. In one case a prisoner was very upset with the judge for not 'listening' to him. In the state of anger he took his slippers and hurled them at the judge. The first slipper fell on the table. He hurled the second slipper at the judge and the second one hit the judge's shoulders. A First Information Report was registered but it was recorded that the slippers hit the clerk and not the judge because of the 'shame' involved in it. It is extreme disrespect to hit someone with a slipper in India. When this prisoner went back to the prison he was not given food for a few days and was denied visits from his family. When he enquired with the Superintendent of the prison about the reason, the Superintendent said that the judge told him orally to punish him this way. The next day he told the judge that he wanted to speak to him but the judge told him that the court would not listen to him anymore and that he ought to listen to the court. This judge continued with the evidence and pronounced the verdict. The prisoner said that the judge should not have continued with the case since he disrespected the person who was in the honourable chair. The co-accused in this same case said that the judge was in an 'angry mood' when he wrote the sentence and if this 'slipper incident' had not happened, they would not have received the death sentence.

One prisoner said that during the court proceedings, the judge dozed off. Furthermore, he said that those who have money were not targeted because they bribed the system and were set free within a year or two. He lamented that it was the poverty-stricken ones who received the death penalty. In one case when the prisoner was given a chance to speak in the end, he appealed to the court that he should be given a chance to live a good life and be a good citizen, because he had an aged and widowed mother and a young wife to look after. However the judge pointed out that it was a shame that he had killed someone and wished to lead a normal family life with his wife and children. In another case, the judge asked the prisoner if he wanted life or the death sentence. He said that he had a little daughter and hence the judge should give him a lesser penalty but he eventually received the death sentence.

The prisoners talked about unfair trials and one of the prisoners said that he asked the judge for an in-camera trial. He was instead issued a 'contempt of court' notice. According to the prisoner, this was because the system did not want an in-camera trial as it could have been used in his appeal process. Another prisoner said that the judge did not allow his lawyer to cross-examine the witnesses. Another prisoner asked for a Central Bureau of Investigation enquiry in his case – 93 murder cases charged against this prisoner and his family. However the court rejected the demand for a Central Bureau of Investigation.

There were also instances where prisoners felt that justice was restored. For instance, a prisoner's wife was arrested along with her children when she came to visit him in the prison. He said that for one month and five days his wife was in police custody and he did not know anything about her whereabouts. When this prisoner was taken to court he told the judge that he had not seen his wife after she was arrested and did not know where she was. The judge said, 'Take him back.' He was taken back to the prison and brought to the court 14 days later and it was the same judge. He reported again that it was 14 days since he had heard from his wife and again the judge said, 'Take him back.' This time he stood there and told the judge, 'This is the place where we can tell our sorrows and pain but nobody wants to listen to us.' He banged his head on the wall. Then the judge asked what was wrong and he told what had happened. After this the judge immediately enquired with the police and found that they were indeed in police lock-up. The judge ordered the wife and children to be presented before the court and they were then transferred to judicial custody the next day. So even though the prisoner had to go to the extent of banging his head, he perceived that he finally found justice in that situation.

Another prisoner said that everything in court was pre-planned because before the case began – the Public Prosecutor, Magistrate and police met in the Magistrate's chamber and decided the outcome beforehand. Another prisoner said that the case was in their favour however the judge was bribed and the decision went against him. Many prisoners said that there was political influence in the decision-making process. For instance one of them said that Kasab's trial affected their cases negatively. Ajmal Kasab, the lone surviving attacker of the Mumbai terror attacks in 2008 was executed in India in November 2012. These prisoners were also accused of terrorism-related crimes and they claimed that their cases were dealt with strictly because of the pressure of the State's ruling party. One prisoner also reported that the court clerk informed him that the judge had taken a bribe therefore he was going to get a death sentence. According to him, he knew beforehand, that he was going to be given the death penalty.

Another actor in this process is the media personnel – the journalists. The media is not independent of the ruling political government, the opposition or other state machineries such as the police and prison. Prisoners said that media never wrote anything 'bad' about judges or lawyers or the police. According to the prisoners, the media wrote the police version of the 'crime'. Some prisoners narrated that their case was so sensationalised that there was a television series or films made out of it. While some prisoners diligently filed articles written about them; others stopped reading them. The prisoner and I disagree with Johnson that our media is 'independent' but certainly agree that it is sensationalistic.[38]

One of the prisoners said that the journalists wanted to take his photograph but did not want to listen to what he had to say. Another prisoner showed me a report about his 'daily routine' in prison. He said that the prison official leaked his information to the journalists and he told the officer, 'You did not do justice to me.' The media branded prisoners calling them *raskshas* (devil), bad person, traitors, Pakistanis, Muslim fundamentalists, hungry wolves and/or sex maniacs. Prisoners also said that the media not only took their photographs but also their children's. This created a stigma for the children in their schools and the society they lived in. Many prisoners also informed me that the media wrote stories about how the prisoners were drug addicts or were into the latest 'fashion'.

Some prisoners also were forced to confess their crimes to a journalist who recorded it and played it on primetime television. One of the prisoners said that the inspector labelled them as 'wild lions hungry to kill people' and that they were people who were 'happy to hear the sound of trickling blood from

38 Unnithan, N. Prabha, ed. *Crime and Justice in India.* New Delhi: SAGE Publications India, 2013.

the murdered victim'. I made a home visit to this prisoner's house. They were extremely poor and did not earn enough even to afford two meals a day. Trial by media is a common factor in cases where the death penalty was awarded. Most of them said that they received the death sentence because of media pressure and circumstantial evidence. Furthermore, another prisoner said that media and India Penal Code should be separate. The only positive account about the media occurred when one of the prisoners said that his family came to know through the papers that he was being transferred from a district prison to a central prison after the death sentence was pronounced. Thus the family could immediately come to the central prison to meet him.

Process 7: Sentenced to Death

During the trial, the death penalty is usually 'demanded' or 'spoken out' in the final argument. A prosecutor for instance argued in the final phase, 'These are wild beasts who cannot be reformed'. Another prosecutor argued, 'They are cold-blooded murderers and if let off free, they would commit murder and rape again'. One set of prisoners said that their lawyers advised them to 'demand' the death sentence on their own because it would be easier to acquit them from a death sentence than from life imprisonment in the High Court. Another prisoner said that the public prosecutor did not call for the death sentence but the judge handed over the punishment anyway. He said that the death sentence should be eliminated from the law as it is biased against minorities in India. He said that 'The minority never gets justice. Rashtriya Swayamsevak Sangh (RSS) and Bharatiya Janata Party (BJP) thinks that every Muslim in India is a terrorist'. He continued that it is not only India that is unjust but also United States. He said that Afro-American people were more likely to be convicted than a white person committing the same crime.

Another prisoner said that his name was found in someone's diary. Therefore, he was implicated in the crime. He said, 'I am a social animal. I have contacts with other people. But just because my name appeared in someone's diary, is that a reason to punish me with death sentence?'

After the final arguments, the judgment is written within two weeks and then judgment is pronounced within a few days. Some prisoners knew from the beginning that they would receive the death penalty while some were caught unaware. In one instance, a prisoner said that, 'If I knew that I was going to be given death sentence, I would have never gone to the court on that day'. Another prisoner said that he was completely shattered upon hearing of his death sentence because contrary to his expectations of a ten year-imprisonment, he got the death sentence. The jailor consoled him in the evening saying that he need not worry and that he could appeal in the High Court.

After the judgment, when the prisoners were brought back from court, they were immediately transferred to a high security yard if they were already in a Central Prison. If they were in a District Prison or Sub-Jail, they were taken to the Central Prison the next day or sometimes even the same evening. Most prisoners had no clue about the procedure after the death sentence was pronounced and many of them thought that they were going to be hanged immediately. One of the prisoners who was in a District Prison was housed in the kitchen after he was given the death sentence as the prison did not have a single-person cell. He said that he was not allowed to meet any of the fellow prisoners; however, when his father came to the prison, he was allowed to meet him in the superintendent's office.

Prisoners narrated the reasons that might have given them death sentence. While some said it was a political decision, others blamed it on their poverty (class) or religion or caste. One prisoner said, 'There is no justice in this country and it is a shame to live in a country like this'. There were prisoners who perceived that they were given a death sentence because they were illiterate and poor. Many of them also questioned the arbitrariness of the death sentence because prisoners who have committed similar crimes were given life sentences and not the death penalty. Another prisoner said that the death sentence should be the same for everyone and not arbitrary; the terms of life sentence should be clearly mentioned as to whether they should be inside the prison for 14 or 20 years and be released after the completion of the term. One of the prisoners on death row asked, 'Why is the law not equal for everyone?' Some prisoners do not know at which stage their cases were – with the President or in the Supreme Court or with the governor. One prisoner said that the criminal nature of people must be dealt within the prison in the form of rehabilitation instead of punishing everyone with a death sentence and that the death sentence has no deterrent effect.

The accused who belonged to the 'rarest of the rare' category or the so-called 'fundamentalist' or 'terrorists' were housed in the high security yard right from the beginning. There were conflicting opinions among the death penalty prisoners about death penalty. One group opined that death penalty should not be removed from law and that when there is a rape and murder, one should get the death penalty. However, another group opposed the death sentence saying that nobody has the power to kill another human being and that judges were not Gods; even they can make mistakes. Some prisoners said that the whole concept of the death penalty is to frighten people and it is not practical. This prisoner was hopeful that he will live tomorrow and that keeps him going. He was just worried that the procedure would take too long.

Thus prisoners confronted the criminal justice system after they were arrested; placed in lock-ups; produced before the magistrate within 24 hours; either sent back to lock-up or judicial custody; sent to judicial custody; trial, being sentenced to death and ending up on the death row.

The Infrastructure of Death Row

Death row is a special city with a life of its own, one that outsiders know nothing about.[39] But prison is also a city which outsiders know nothing about. When one reaches a prison, one cannot miss the tri-colour (the Indian Flag) in front of the prison. This symbolises the power of the State over this institution. When I visited any prison for the first time I asked the officials if I could visit the whole prison. This was to observe and understand the structure and function of different units of the prison. I was taken to all the places in a prison where 'normal' visitors were taken. This included observing the barracks from outside, the kitchen, library and work sheds. Except for prisons in two states – Kerala and Assam; none of the officers agreed to show me the 'gallows', the assumption being women are '*weak*' and should not see or would not bear to see these 'terrible' things.

Main Gate

One enters a prison through a wicket-gate which is part of the main gate. The wicket-gate is 0.6 metre in width and 1.5 metres in height and the main gate is approximately three metres wide and four metres high. The gates is usually painted with colours identical to that of the departmental flag if prescribed by the State Government and these gates are made up of strong steel or iron frames with vertical round or square steel bars of 25mm. diameter. An officer informed me that the dimension of both gates should be wide enough for transporting a fire truck, in case of fire or a lorry for transporting raw materials/logs for the factory. One has to pass your identity cards through the peephole on the wicket-gate. A guard verifies it and opens the wicket-gate. As soon as one enters the main gate, one can see a very similar gate with a wicket door 12–14 metres away. The space between these two gates functioned as the reception area. The main purpose of this reception area is to track prisoners and visitors who enter and leave the prison. On either side of the reception desks there are steps leading to offices which could be Superintendent's offices or the judicial record sections. The main gate is opened only when an official of high rank enters the prison. Thus Superintendents, magistrates, judges have the privilege of entering the prison without bending down. Everyone else entering through the wicket-gate has to bend down and enter. Guards informed me that 'Officers cannot bend down because it is a dishonour to bend down; that is the reason the main gate is opened for them'. This has been a custom since colonial times. I wondered if it implied that everyone who entered through the wicket-gate is dishonoured. Entry into the prison is only

39 Jackson, Bruce. *Fieldwork*. Urbana: University of Illinois Press, 1987.

through a single point, that is the main gate and all other entry points, even if they exist are closed permanently.

Once I was inside the gate, I was asked to write my name and address in the register which maintains the records of everyone going 'in' and 'out' of the prison. When I left the prison, I had to sign my 'out' time against my 'in' time. This showed the number of hours I was inside the prison and it also was to make sure that I indeed 'left' the prison. One is also asked to leave mobile phones at the reception area. Every prison has main gates and huge walls separating them from the normal population so that no-one can 'escape' the prison. In the reception area, there is a blackboard which shows the prison population. The table below depicts a typical display board in a prison. Prisoners are counted every morning and evening. The guards informed me that the main gate and second gate are never opened at the same time to prevent prisoners from escaping. In spite of the security, whenever I visited the prisons, there was at least one prisoner recorded in the escape column. This board also indicates the authorised accommodation capacity. All prisons I visited had more prisoners than the authorised capacity.

Table 3.2 Typical display board in a prison

Sr. No.	Men	Women
IPC Section 302 (murder)		
Undertrials		
Death sentence convicts		
Detainees		
Escaped		
Authorised capacity		
Total		

Belongings in Prison

Once the accused comes to the prison, s/he is given a plate, glass, blanket, sheets and a pillow. Convicts are given two set of clothes or what is known as 'prison uniform' and undertrials are allowed to wear their own clothes. This meant that death row prisoners are given prison uniforms but as undertrials they could wear their own clothes. Usually they are also given mugs for showering or using the toilet however some prisoners reported that they used the same bowl for food and going to the toilet as they are not provided with different ones.

Barracks

The accommodation of prisoners is categorised according to age group and criminal background. A repeat offender is never placed with a first time offender. Young prisoners between 18 and 21 years are housed in '*Baba*' (new born baby) barrack while prisoners older than 55 years in '*Budha*' (old man) barrack. Barracks have an accommodation capacity of more than 50 prisoners. The age group between 22 and 55 years are placed in normal barracks. However, this also depends on the number of prisoners in the prisons. There is a problem of overcrowding in all prisons in India. Where the crime is high profile, prisoners are housed in single cells or high-security yards. Most death row convicts in terrorist related crimes are housed in a high-security yard from the beginning. Prisoners on death row who are not in such high-profile cases are housed in normal barracks when they are undertrials.

The barracks are similar to the society outside – in the centre are the economically 'rich' and high-profile prisoners; to the margins where the toilets were or where the floor was damp were the economically 'poor', tribal or the lower-caste prisoners. The minimum height of roofs or ceilings in a barrack is not less than 10 feet from the floor. The floor of the barrack is made of impermeable material such as cement. All barracks have verandas which are generally two metres in width. Though ventilation of the sleeping barracks is of the greatest importance, prisoners are not permitted to close the windows and ventilation openings at their discretion. The ventilation is however controlled according to the season whenever necessary. The lights in the barrack are not turned off during the night for security reasons.

Toilets and Bathrooms

Each barrack has a water-closet, urinals and wash-places attached to it. However, the ratio of toilets to prisoners is low. The partitions separating the latrines are high enough to provide a reasonable degree of privacy. However, they do not have regular doors. The doors are open on top. This is to avoid suicides or fights. For bathing, some prisons had cubicles, while some had a common tub made out of cement filled with water. Prisoners drew water from the tub and showered in the open. This was the case for both men and women. There was also a shortage of water in the prison during summer which led to various skin diseases as a result of poor hygiene.

Kitchen

The kitchen is located at a central place inside the prisons so that the distribution of food among the prisoners is convenient. None of the kitchens are built close to the sleeping barracks. Exhaust fans are installed and artificial ventilation is provided in some prisons. Prison manuals of all states mention that the management of kitchen or cooking of food on caste or religious basis is prohibited in the prison. Some kitchens use firewood as fuel to cook while most of the prison kitchen has cooking gas. The breakfast preparations begin at 2:00 a.m. or 3:00 a.m. Lunch preparations begin immediately after breakfast is served at 7:00 a.m. Lunch in every prison is served at 10:00 a.m. or 10:30 a.m. The evening tea and dinner preparations begin immediately after lunch is served and dinner is distributed at 4:00 p.m.

Hospitals

Every central prison has a hospital attached to it with a limited number of beds for indoor treatment with separate wards for men and women. The location of the hospital is far away from the barracks. Every hospital ward is constructed to allow for sufficient light and air. Latrines and baths are provided close to the wards so that sick prisoners would not have to walk far to use them. There is generally an arrangement for continuous supply of portable water in the hospitals.

Work Sheds

There are work sheds in all central prison, though the nature of work in these sheds depends on the availability of resources. For instance, in the North-East of India where bamboo is available, cane-work is common. In Western India, prisoners do tailoring and carpentry. Women in all these central prisons were hardly given any work. Their task is to cut vegetables for the prison kitchen. There were also work-sheds in women's prisons but these are non-functional. There are recreation facilities for prisoners in their yards. In some prisons, the prisoners used the ground space to play volleyball or other outdoor games. All prisons have a library which the prisoners said have outdated books. There are also auditoriums in each prison for cultural programmes and yoga.

Death Row

Death row is a prison within a prison – physically and socially isolated from the prison community and the outside world.[40] It is the cell or block of cells in which prisoners condemned to death are held while awaiting execution. They are known by different names such as *Andheri* (darkness) yard, separate yard, high security, '*phasi* (hanging) yard' or '*phasiwale* (hanging people) yard'. The death

40 Schabas, William. *The Death Penalty as Cruel Treatment and Torture: Capital Punishment Challenged in the World's Courts*. Boston, MA: Northeastern University Press, 1996.

row differs from the rest of the prison because the row was the single place where the rhetoric of rehabilitation was meaningless (one was there waiting to die, not trying to be improved) and where the rhetoric of punishment was inappropriate (the punishment was not time served on the row but execution). It is a place that is not covered in any way by the usual set of rules. Prisoners live here for years while the legal system decides whether they could be killed or re-sentenced to a prison term or set free.[41]

Death row prisoners are normally segregated from other convicts serving fixed terms of imprisonment and the reason for this is somewhat obscure. One of the reasons could be that the individual is already a 'dead man' and thus no longer belongs with the living. Another explanation could be the threat to the security of other prisoners and prison guards, from desperate individuals who have literally nothing to lose.[42] But this also emerges from one the principles of prisons – isolation. Prisoners should be kept in isolation so that they can be reformed;[43] but it is an irony in itself when it comes to death row prisoners because they are sentenced to death because they 'cannot' be or are 'incapable' of reform.

Cells in Death Row

Cells inside a death row are built on a raised platform. For instance in one of the prisons there are five cells in a row built on a raised platform and opposite to this row would be another row with five cells built similarly. There is usually a ground between these two rows of cells. It has essentially three elements – a toilet, a bed made out of concrete and a ventilator. There is no furniture in the cell. The door has iron bars which can be locked and the cell is lit at night. The toilets were in working condition according to them. The poor prisoners clean the toilets of rich prisoners and in return receive goodies from the prison canteen. Most prisoners have pictures of god/goddesses on their walls.

The cells are hot in the summer and cold in the winter, cramped and barren. The stone and steel cellblock seemed to express the full nature of imprisonment as seen in the popular fancy. The dimension of the cell is the alpha and omega of life in prison. Like many animals in their cages, the prison population is an aggregate rather than a social group, a mass of isolates rather than a society.[44] Similar to how Sykes describes, prisoners on death row stated that the temperature in the cell was very hot during summer, wet during the

41 Jackson, Bruce. *Fieldwork.*

42 Schabas, William. *The Death Penalty as Cruel Treatment and Torture.*

43 Foucault, Michel. *Discipline and Punish.*

44 Sykes, Gresham M. *The Society of Captives: A Study of a Maximum Security Prison.* Princeton: Princeton University Press, 1958.

monsoon and cold during winter. All the prisoners were allowed to listen to a common radio, read books and write letters to their families. There was often space in front of the single cells where prisoners could exercise. There were no fans in any of the cells because there was a fear among the authorities that the prisoners might commit suicide if there was a fan in the cell. They also had a bag with their meagre belongings. The prisoners had their files which were found in the cell usually. There were very few prisoners who left their files with the prison authorities in the 'judicial department' at the main gate.

High Security Yard

The high security yard is very similar to 'super maximum custody'; colloquially known as *supermax* in the United States. Maximum security prison represents a social system in which an attempt is made to create and maintain total or almost total social control.[45] Prisoners in supermax facilities usually held in single cell lock-down, commonly referred to as solitary confinement. Congregate activities with other prisoners are prohibited; other prisoners cannot even be seen from another prisoner's cell. Communication with other prisoners is prohibited or difficult (for example, shouting from one cell to the other cell is prohibited); visiting and telephone privileges were limited.[46]The main elements in a supermax custody is that accommodation is physically separate, or at least separable, from other units or facilities, in which a controlled environment emphasising safety and security, via restricted movement and separation from staff and other prisoners is provided for. It was for prisoners who were identified through an administrative rather than a disciplinary process who needed such control on the grounds of their violent or seriously disruptive behaviour in other high security facilities.[47]

The segregation of one person from the others and to be all alone in a single cell is solitary confinement. The 'separate system', the 'silent system', 'the hole' and other variants possess the same vice. The separate confinement of a person with occasional access of other persons is also solitary confinement. In a general sense, it means the separate confinement of a prisoner, with only occasional access to any other person and that would be only at the discretion of the jailor. Confinement inside a prison does not necessarily import cellular isolation. Indeed, in a jail, cells were ordinarily occupied by more than one inmate

45 Ibid.

46 Fellner, Jamie and Mariner, Joanne. *Cold Storage: Super-maximum Security Confinement in Indiana.* Human Rights Watch, 1997. See http://www.hrw.org/reports/1997/usind/ (last accessed 31 July 2015).

47 King, Roy D. 'The rise and rise of Supermax an American Solution in search of a problem?' *Punishment & Society* 1, no. 2 (1999): 163–86.

and community life inside dormitories and cells is common. Therefore, 'to be confined in a cell' did not mean that the confinement should be in a solitary cell. Solitary confinement could only be imposed by the court according to Indian laws. However, based on the Prisons Act, 1894[48] and the Indian Penal Code, 1860,[49] prisoners are placed in singular confinement. A court decision spelled out that this was a subversion of statutory provisions whereby a disciplinary variant of solitary confinement is clamped down on a prisoner by an executive officer.[50]

There was a certain prisoner who said that when he was initially brought to death row, he was allowed outside his cell for five minutes only. The rest of the time, he used to sit and cry. Then finally the other prisoners told the officers that he might go mad if he is not allowed to move about freely. That is when, according to the prisoner, the guards started allowing him out of solitary confinement for longer periods of time. However sometimes when he cried, the guards said, 'Oh well, he has started his daily drama'. There were prisoners who have been in a single cell for over 17 years. A so-called 'terrorist' was placed in a high security prison in a cell called the '*Anda*' (Egg) Barrack. It is a barrack in the shape of an egg for the so-called 'high profile criminals'. According to him the *Anda* (Egg) Barrack is the most inconvenient thing built for human beings. He said, 'These cells are meant for one person and usually there is an average of five persons in one cell. We must be given animal rights and not human rights because animals are treated better than us'.

The only woman on death row whom I had interviewed for this study said that during the day she is out with the other women but at night, she is in a separate cell and feels very scared. She said that she chanted the name of God at night and tried to go to sleep. Every 15 days she met her husband for 5 to15 minutes on death row where the men were housed. She said that the lady officers asked her to remove her greens bangles which are a symbol of a married woman; but she did not. She told them that her husband was not dead. This lady held my hands and asked me, 'Do you think I can kill so many people? Do you think I am dangerous?' After the interview with this woman prisoner, the lady officer told me her version, 'This woman has killed so and so number of people, she is very dangerous and utterly stubborn' I did not find her 'dangerous' instead I found her very endearing. She would greet me in this manner: 'The Good Morning Madam'.

While a death row cell is a space of their own, prisoners reported feeling suffocated being locked up for 23 hours a day. They were brought out of their cells for half an hour in the morning and half an hour in the evening. This is the

48 Prisons Act, 1894 (Section 30 (2)).

49 Indian Penal Code, 1860 (Section 73 and 74).

50 Sunil Batra v Delhi Administration 1980 AIR 1579, 1980 SCR (2) 557.

maximum period they were allowed to be out. Due to these rules many call this situation a '*jail ke andhar jail*' (Jail within a jail). These were the exact words that death row prisoners from Texas used while describing in the 1980s.[51] Another prisoner said 'There are rules for sports, food, bathroom and toilet. We want freedom inside the jail. When we want to learn yoga; we are harassed. The moment we are given death sentence, we should be hanged; so that at least we don't face this harassment'.

Overcrowding in prisons is very common but it was truly unheard of that death row was also overcrowded. In some prisons, a death row cell confined four people at a time. A prisoner told me, 'Madam, it is crowded but whom do we tell this to or who wants to listen to our overcrowding problems'? According to a prison official, there were cases where prisoners from the same 'case/gang' were placed in different prisons in the same state to avoid fights between them or to divide them with the aim to 'split' their strength. Another prisoner said that the cell and the yard resemble a '*khandar*' (ruined fort) especially because once a rat came and took his *roti* (Indian bread).

Prisoners have expressed their discontent over the nomenclature for this yard. It is called *Andheri* (darkness) yard because it is a yard where condemned prisoners are housed and the ones who should not see the light of the day because they are condemned to death. The name 'separate yard' exists because this yard is separate from the rest of the prisoners for security reasons or to differentiate between condemned, convicted and undertrial prisoners. It gets the name 'high security yard' because the place is highly secured due to the presence of high profile prisoners such as death penalty prisoners or political prisoners or undertrials arrested for 'serious' criminal cases. A prisoner from the 'Andheri' (darkness) yard while describing his difficulty in coping with the yard said, '*Andheri mein gum, duniya se door tabhi hotha jab usko kabar mein uthara jatha hai. Humko kabar mein zinda rakha hai*'. It means people are lost in the darkness and become distant from the living world when they are placed in the grave. The prisoner opined that that with the special (grave) yard, the death row prisoners are kept alive in a grave.

Life on Death Row

The everyday life of prisoners includes their daily routine, the rules they have to follow, their perceptions of prison officials and prisons as an institution, of co-prisoners, their relatives and their experience and perception of the treatment they receive as prisoners on death row. One of the characteristics of total

51 Jackson, Bruce. *Fieldwork.*

institutions is that there is a strict discipline with how the institution functions.[52] As a part of total institutions, prisoners have to follow certain timings in prison and follow a strict regime. Loss of agency forms an integral part of this process. Agency is 'the capacity, condition or state of acting or exerting power.[53] Prisoners steadily lose their capacity to exert power and control their destiny as they serve time in prison. Prison life is completely routinised and restricted, with few opportunities to make decisions or exert choice in their daily routine.[54] Some prisoners elaborated upon common rules governing them while some spoke of exceptional rules followed in particular prisons. One thing to remember while reading this should be that a prisoner is not a prisoner 'under the sentence of death' unless all the appeals are exhausted or petitions rejected.[55]

Daily Routine

The day begins with waking up at 5:30 a.m. The warder who is a trusted prisoner on duty unlocks the cells in the presence of a jailor or an assistant jailor. This is followed by the counting of prisoners. During this time the prisoners fold their beddings. They clean their cells and perform their morning ablutions. At around 6:30 a.m. breakfast is served. The food served depends on the region where the prison is located and the food is according to the staple food of that region. For instance in Maharashtra, a typical breakfast would include flattened rice or *Sabudana khichadi* (sago). Convicted prisoners begin their daily work at around 9:00 a.m. but since death row prisoners are not allowed to work they spend their time in their cells. At around 9:00 a.m. there is a 'round' by a senior prison officer. 'Rounds' are regular visits conducted every morning by the Superintendent or the Senior Jailor of each prison. This is a time to inspect the barracks and cells of prisoners and it is usually done in the morning. During the rounds, the prisoners also have the opportunity to talk about their grievances and petitions to the officer. This is the time when the officer checks if the prisoners have petitions or grievances. After the rounds, the prisoners are in lock-up again. In some prisons they are unlocked separately for half an hour in the morning and are allowed to exercise outside their cells while in some prisons, prisoners are allowed outside their cells all day except during *bandi* which literally means 'being closed'. *Bandi* time for all prisons across India

---

52 Goffman, Erving. 'On the characteristics of total institutions'.

53 Babcock, Philip. *Webster's Third New International Dictionary*. Springfield: G & C Merriam Company, 1971.

54 Irwin, John and Barbara Owen. 'Harm and the contemporary prison' , in Liebling, Alison and Shadd Maruna, eds. *The Effects of Imprisonment*. Cullompton: Willan, 2005: 94–117.

55 Sunil Batra v Delhi Administration 1980 AIR 1579, 1980 SCR (2) 557.

is from 12:00 p.m. to 3:00 p.m. In the afternoon, at 3.00 p.m. prisoners are again taken out one at a time for walks or are all allowed out in the yard at the same time. At 5:30 p.m. a bell is rung which indicates the closing of the cells of the prison. Prisoners are counted and are asked to go into their respective cells. After they are back in the cells, they are released the next morning at 5:30 a.m. and the same routine continues.

Rules on Death Row

Concurrently, there are certain rules that prisoners on death row have to follow. These rules are arbitrary and vary from prison to prison. In all prisons, according to the rules, death row prisoners are not allowed to work like other convicted prisoners and do not have concrete ways to engage themselves in any other activity. Therefore, it is the up to the discretion of the individuals to decide the mode of spending time. The status of their case plays a big role in determining the activities that the prisoners would engage in. The ones whose cases were in the High Court were restless and hardly found the motivation to do anything such as reading or writing. This was similar for the ones who had their Mercy Petitions with the President or the Governor of the State. The ones who had their cases in the Supreme Court were a bit more relaxed than the others as this takes a long time. Some of them learned English from fellow prisoners but most of the time they sat idle or read their case-papers. Most prisoners said that their daily routine only had one activity apart from walking for half an hour outside their cells- 'reading newspapers or listening to the daily newspaper being read'. However, some prisoners have written and published novels, stories and diaries in regional languages.

With regard to prison uniform, prisoners sentenced to death follow certain norms. For example, prisoners on death row are not allowed to wear 'coloured-dress' but only white. In India, white is a colour worn for mourning as opposed to black in other cultures. As undertrials they wear civil clothes in the prison. Some other rules that were given to them upon arrival in the high security yard were that they had to stay within the gate of the high security yard. They are asked to stay within the cell when authorities come and after the authorities leave, prisoners can come out again. Furthermore, they were told that they could not move without the permission of the authority. Concerning visitors, they were told that only blood relatives could meet them. In some prisons they were told that they could eat 'as much as' they wanted. One of the death row prisoners said that when he was brought to death row from another prison, his fellow prisoners cautioned him that he would not be allowed to use his reading glasses on death row. He, therefore, did not bring his reading glasses with him. He suffers from constant headache because of that. In some prisons, they were allowed to listen to the radio. Some of them said, 'For us prisoners, there are no fundamental rights in reality'. This prisoner also said that when he came to the prison first he did not know of any rules and when he and his co-accused asked for clarification, they were immediately transferred because they were 'trouble makers'. He continued that it was only the '*khaki*' (police-uniform) which could make and break rules.

Another phenomenon that occurred as a routine in their prison life was being branded or labelled. Some of the names given to them by the media, police and prosecutors stuck to them. They were called 'Muslim fundamentalist', '*Samaj ke liye khatharnak*' (dangerous element for the society), '*doshdrohi*' (traitors), '*Pakistanis*' and 'hungry wolves'. I was introduced to a prisoner whose first name was '*Kothi*'. I learned from my translator that it meant a monkey. I asked for his 'real' name and he said it was 'Mr. A'. He said that he was addressed by that name because according to the authorities he 'resembled' a monkey and he 'behaved' like one. When I addressed him by his actual first name, the guard told me, 'Madam his name is Kothi and not Mr. A' and laughed hysterically. To that, Mr. A immediately responded, 'You (system) have given me this name Kothi. I am not a Kothi, I am not a monkey'.

Hunger Strike

Facilities such as phones, television, radio and books were a privilege rather than a right for the prisoners on death row. In some prisons, death row prisoners are allowed to make phone calls to their families but this facility did not come to them easily. Prisoners had to go on a hunger strike to obtain these facilities. Some prisoners said that when they went on a hunger strike, the prison authorities told them, 'You want to fast? Go ahead! You will die and we will say that you died on your way to the hospital. We do not care about your hunger strike'. Hunger strikes have been used frequently by the prisoners to express their dissent. Gandhi often used this weapon against the state to voice his dissent against the Raj (British Empire). Today it is Irom Sharmila who has been on a fast for the past 14 years to repeal the 'draconian law'. It is called the Armed Forces (Special Powers) Act, 1958 which gives the army (troops) the right to shoot anyone suspected of being a rebel and to arrest suspected militants without a warrant. Irom has been fasting for the past 14 years to get this Act repealed. Similarly, some of the prisoners on death row who were in the last stage of their mercy petition went on a hunger strike. For instance, one prisoner was disappointed with the fact that he had spent 15 years on the death row and there was no response to his mercy petition. He held a hunger strike for four months. The authorities tried to force-feed him. They could not succeed. Then there was a second phase of hunger strike. This time the Inspector General of Prisons and the Superintendent convinced him to abandon the hunger strike so that he could be alive and healthy to receive pardon for his death penalty, if it is granted. There was another instance where prisoners used their bodies as a weapon to claim their right. A certain prisoner on death row had serious kidney problems and the prison officials did not take him to the hospital even after he pleaded with them. This prisoner became seriously ill one day and still he was not taken to the hospital. So all the prisoners on death row in this particular prison went on a hunger strike and the prisoner with the kidney problem was taken to hospital immediately. According to the prisoners, when prisoners refuse food as a group, the prison officials have to write a report to the higher authorities. So to avoid this, they listen to the prisoners' petitions.

Food in Prison

While describing the food received in prison, all prisoners echoed the opinion that the food was 'ok' but only if their minds were 'ok' could they eat something. Most of them said that even when they were given good food they were not in the right state of mind to eat it. Some said that they did not have an appetite because whenever they tried to eat, they thought about their families and wondered if they had food to eat or if they were starving. Another prisoner said that he had no appetite but he ate everything because everything was equally tasteless. There were also prisoners who said that the food given to a mad dog was better than the food they were served on the death row because the food sometimes contained maggots and worms. There was a set of prisoners who were happy to receive food and even enjoyed it. They said that, 'When we are outside, we are so poor and do not eat food every day. Here we get food everyday'. There is also a 'gossip' among prisoners that the food is mixed with sedatives (drugs) so that they sleep at night and the prison officials are not 'disturbed'.

Rehabilitation

Receiving education in the prison is a part of the rehabilitation and reformation process of prison. However this argument falls short in case of death row prisoners because according to the system, prisoners on death row can neither be 'reformed' nor be 'rehabilitated'. Access to education was a struggle for some prisoners on death row. One of the prison Superintendents said, 'You are prisoners waiting to be hanged – there is no need to study'. There were also prisons where the death row prisoners were not allowed to study. However, most of the prisons allowed educational facilities to prisoners on death row. Some prisoners who were completely illiterate learned from their co-prisoners who could read and write. There is a prison canteen in every prison and all prisoners have access to the canteen including prisoners on death row. They could buy various items from the canteen using their own money. The maximum amount of money that the prisoners can receive is Rs. 200/- (Euro 3 or 4 approximately) from their families as money orders. However, most of them did not receive any money because of their family's financial situation or because they lost contact with their family.

Treatment on Death Row

One of the prisoners died on death row during the research period and the reason for his death was 'natural causes' according to the prison. This deceased prisoner had told me that he had a major heart ailment, was hypertensive and diabetic. He also had a spine disorder and suffered severe backache. His eyesight was very poor due to diabetes. He showed me the reports from the Civil Hospital. He said that, 'A beggar on the street outside is treated better than a prisoner on death row'. Out of the 16 prisons I visited, only one prison had a psychiatrist who visited the prisoners on death row every week. This doctor told me that prisoners generally do not have physical illness; most of their illnesses were psychological in nature. In one prison, a prisoner said that they were given sleeping tablets so that prison authorities were not 'disturbed' at night. This prisoner told me that he stored all these tablets because according to him these tablets were administered to 'mad men' and he did not want to eat tablets given to 'mad men'. I asked him if there was no checking in his cell anytime because according to the prison rules, cells were checked on a regular basis. He said that there was no checking in the cells whatsoever and even if there was a checking he managed to hide them. Prisoners reported that they did not like going to the prison hospital as the doctors gave the same medicine for every illness.

Another prisoner said that when a person comes to the prison with a death sentence, s/he should be hanged immediately and not made to wait for their death. Talking about fellow death row prisoners, one of the prisoners said that fellow prisoners understand each other very well because of all them receive more or less similar treatment from the criminal justice system. They said that there were hardly any fights among them. Another prisoner added that since they did not know who dies or lives next, they remained cordial with each other.

One of the prisoners said that they were not treated in a humane manner. They often felt humiliated with the way the prison officials spoke to them. Prison officials had a different view about taking care of prisoners on death row. One of the prison officials said that in his three years of service in that particular prison, he hoped that he would not have to do anything with the gallows. Prison officials are transferred within the state every three years and this officer wanted to be transferred soon as he did not want blood on his hands. In contrast to this, another prison official said, 'We once prepared everything for a prisoner to be hanged and then these human rights people intervened and stopped the execution. I was so sad that the execution did not take place'.

In another instance, after an interview with the prisoners, the Superintendent asked me my opinion about the prisoners whom I had interviewed. I said that I could not assess them so quickly. The official told me, 'Madam, they are hard-core criminals who are never going to change. You are blind not to see it'. Another prison officer told me, 'You do not see them every day; you see them sometimes; we deal with them every day and we know how 'dangerous' they are. You don't realise it'. One of the prisoners said, '*British jamane ka jailors hai. humko andhere mein rakhthe hai aur hamare haqko ke baare mein hame nahi bathathe hai*' (The jail staff are like jailors of British Raj (Era). They keep us in the dark and do not inform us about our rights.)

One of the prisoners said that prison as a whole does not give you any respect or dignity and that one needs to have dignity over oneself and no one else. Prisoners used the following words *shoshan, bigaad deth ihai, shaanti nahi dethi, disturb karthi hai, bhrashtachar, samaj ke layak nahi rahatha* (Torture, destroys you, does not give you peace, disturbs you, full of corruption, does not leave you fit to be back in society). Another prisoner said that not even in one's dreams should one go to a place like a prison. He said that in prison, they were not human beings but just a number. Similarly another prisoner said that he did not know how to survive but he is still surviving each day. He said that nobody looks into their circumstances and as prisoners on death row they were not fighting with a single person but a whole community. Another prisoner added '*Yaha rehena hi muskhil hogaya hai*' (it has become difficult to survive in the prison). On being asked about his living on the death row a prisoner said, 'Be locked inside for a month, get third class treatment, no medication, do not meet anyone – then you'll know how it is to survive the death row'. Similarly another prisoner said, 'Lifers have a life even inside the prison but we on death row do not. We have no freedom, no timing, we do not know what to do'.

Death Row Syndrome or Phenomenon

The 'death row phenomenon' or 'death row syndrome' is a combination of circumstances found on death row that produce severe mental trauma and physical deterioration in prisoners under those sentences. This phenomenon is a result of the harsh conditions experienced on death row, the length of time that they have experienced and the anxiety of awaiting one's own execution.[56] Classic studies from Camus's *Reflections from the Guillotine*, Foucault's and Jeremy

56 Hudson, Patrick. 'Does the death row phenomenon violate a prisoner's human rights under international law?' *European Journal of International Law* 11, no. 4 (2000): 833–56.

Bentham's works demonstrate the experiences of being on death row.[57] They document the nature and problems of being on death row. Although varied in their approaches, each of these classical works offers a glimpse of the wider social structures within which death row prisoners were positioned. Apart from these classical studies there are numerous scholars who have documented this severe mental trauma, a result of the stress associated with death sentences.[58]

Specific manifestations included an overwhelming sense of fear and helplessness, mental incompetence, fluctuating moods, recurrent depression, mental slowness, confusion, forgetfulness, lethargy, listlessness, drowsiness, symptoms of senility (in the form of rambling correspondence, misplacing objects within a small cell and expressing disconnected thoughts), self-mutilation and insanity.[59] Other associated factors that contribute to the mental trauma included a cramped environment of deprivation, arbitrary rules, harassment and isolation from others.[60] The conditions of confinement also appear to aggravate

---

57 Camus, Albert. *Reflections on the Guillotine.* Indiana: Fridtjof-Karla Publications, 1960; Foucault, Michel. *Discipline and Punish*; Bentham, Jeremy. *An Introduction to the Principles of Morals and Legislation (Collected Works of Jeremy Bentham).* Oxford: Clarendon Press, 1996.

58 Some of the scholars who have written about death row phenomenon include Schabas, William. 'Developments in Criminal Law and Criminal Justice: Execution Delayed, Execution Denied'. *Criminal Law Forum* 5 (1994): 180–788; Radelet, Michael. *Facing the Death Penalty: Essays on a Cruel and unusual Punishment.* Philadelphia: Temple University Press, 1990; Mello, Michael. 'Facing death alone: The post-conviction attorney crisis on death row'. *American University Law Review* 37 (1987): 513–607; Strafer, G. Richard. 'Volunteering for execution: Competency, voluntariness and the propriety of third party intervention'. *Journal of Criminal Law and Criminology* 74 (1983): 860–912; Holland, Nancy. 'Death row conditions: Progression toward constitutional protections'. *Akron Law Review* 19 (1985): 293–310; Johnson, Robert. 'Under sentence of death: The psychology of death row confinement'. *Law & Psychology Review* 5 (1979): 141–92; Hussain, Abdul H. and Tozman Seymour. 'Psychiatry on death row'. *Journal of Clinical Psychiatry* 39, no. 3 (1978): 183–8; West, Louis Jolyon. 'Psychiatric reflections on the death penalty'. *American Journal of Orthopsychiatry* 45, no. 4 (1975): 689–700; Gallemore, Johnnie L., H. James Panton and Edward Kaufman. 'Inmate responses to lengthy death row confinement'. *The American Journal of Psychiatry* 129, no. 2 (1972): 167–72; Bluestone, Harvey and L. Carl McGahee. 'Reaction to extreme stress: Impending death by execution'. *The American Journal of Psychiatry* 119, no. 5 (1962): 393–6.

59 Blank, Stephen. 'Killing time: The process of waiving appeal—The Michael Ross death penalty cases'. *Journal of Law & Policy* 14 (2006): 735–77; Cunningham, Mark D. and Mark P. Vigen. 'Death row inmate characteristics, adjustment and confinement: A critical review of the literature'. *Behavioural Sciences & the Law* 20, no. 1-2 (2002): 191–210; Strafer, G. Richard. 'Volunteering for execution.

60 Cunningham, Mark D. and Mark P. Vigen. 'Death row inmate characteristics, adjustment and confinement.

existing mental disorders.[61] Jurists have also noted the debilitating mental effects of sentencing a person to death. A United States Court (California) stated the process of carrying out a verdict of death is frequently so degrading to the human spirit as to constitute 'psychological torture'.[62] In India, commenting on a prisoner who had been on death row for many years, a judge noted that the person would be more of a vegetable than a person and hanging a vegetable is not the death penalty.[63]

Length of Time Experienced

The death row phenomenon was first described internationally in the Soering case.[64] Very recently it was Abu-Jamal who described the death row phenomenon.[65] The death row phenomenon as a violation of human rights and has been well-expounded in various literatures including many court judgments both in international law and national law.[66] Prisoners go through this feeling of being killed every second on death row. The wait for their appeals makes them anxious and nervous thus violating their right to be free from this mental torture. Many countries for this reason do not extradite prisoners to countries which carry out the death penalty. However, Germany violated this law by sending back a prisoner who sought asylum and was sentenced to death in 2001. His sentence was only commuted to life in March 2014. Devinder was not part of this study and hence I mention his name.[67] While the delay in judicial processes itself is an insufficient ground for causing death row phenomenon, the supplementing factors of mental agony and perceptions of harsh treatment while being on death row are enough reason to consider a more humane approach to deal with prisoners on death row. The 111 prisoners interviewed in this study have been waiting from 5 to 17 years on death row. However they have been incarcerated for longer – the longest for over 22 years. One of the prisoners who has been incarcerated for 10–12 years and who has been on death row for eight years says that he has been writing to the Government of India and the Human Rights Commission of India about his innocence. No one has responded and he felt as if he was being treated as garbage. He said that they should get a chance to

61 Ibid.

62 People v Anderson, 6 cal 3d 628, 649 (1971); see also Soering v United Kingdom, 161 Eur.Ct. H.R. (Ser.A) 34, (1989) 11 EHRR 439.

63 Rajendra Prasad v State of Uttar Pradesh 1979 AIR 916, 1979 SCR (3) 78.

64 Soering v United Kingdom, 161 Eur.Ct. H.R. (Ser.A) 34, (1989) 11 EHRR 439.

65 Abu-Jamal, Mumia. *Live from Death Row*. Harper Perennial, 1996.

66 Soering v United Kingdom, 161 Eur.Ct. H.R. (Ser.A) 34, (1989) 11 EHRR 439; Triveniben v State of Gujrat, (1988) 4 AScc 574; (1989) 1 SCC, 678.

67 State of Punjab v Devinder Pal Singh Bhullar & Ors. etc., AIR 2012 SC 364.

prove their innocence and secure a chance to get justice. Another prisoner who was in the prison for 20 years altogether and 15 years on the death row said the law should be equal for everyone.

Similarly another prisoner said that at every point his case got worse and his charge sheet was 15,000 pages long. He said that even if he appeals it would take him such a long time and there would be no end to his case. He further added that by then he will be old or rather felt old already. He said poignantly that his youth and family life was annihilated in the four walls of the prison because the system did not want to listen to the truth.

One of the other prisoners said that he had never had a criminal record; however, crime was a 'good thing' for the police because they got promoted after 'solving' these 'gruesome' crimes. He also said that he hailed from a poor family and was being mentally tortured on death row. He posed an almost rhetorical question concerning the time that he would have to live on death row, adding that the uncertainty of being on death row kills them every day. Another prisoner who differentiated between life sentence prisoners and death row prisoners said that life sentence prisoners knew when they will leave the prison or a person who has committed theft knows s/he is going to be out in five years but according to him death penalty prisoners do not know when or if they were going to be released at all. He said that, 'I feel that there is no going forward from death sentence other than death itself'.

Mercy petitions were written by prisoners who could write in English or an NGO representative who wrote on their behalf. One of the prisoners said that the system or the President of India is an inefficient scavenger because s/he is unable to clean the mess in the Indian Judicial System which is like a clogged latrine. Another prisoner questioned why the President took such a long time to decide about death penalty cases. He continued that the waiting period was long and one died a thousand times a year. At the same time some were full of remorse about their crimes. Prisoners who have reached the mercy petition stage said that they have terrible panic problems, feel worn-out, suffer from acute depression and lose tremendous amount of weight. Prisoners have further added that they have felt suicidal. Besides that they also possess feelings of anger, confusion, sadness, restlessness and guilt. Finally a prisoner added that everyone had the capacity to change and that even prisoners on death row should be given a chance to prove oneself in society.

Anxiety of Awaiting One's Own Execution

When prisoners on death row were placed in solitary confinement, they felt very uncomfortable. Some said that they tried to keep themselves calm by praying and meditating however all of them said that they have lost their peace of mind. There was a certain prisoner who also asked for conjugal rights because he reasoned that someone had to carry on the family if he is executed. Almost all prisoners said that they could not sleep during the night. Many said that they only slept for half an hour and were awake most of the night. Therefore, it was very common for them to consume sleeping tablets. Many prisoners broke down while narrating their lives to me. Some claimed that they were innocent and had been framed; some cried because they felt guilty about the crime; some cried thinking about their families; some cried talking about their broken lives. One of the other prisoners broke down saying that he did not mean to kill, it happened on the spur of the moment and he regretted it. One prisoner said that the most difficult part of staying on death row was that he constantly thought about his parents. He also claimed to be innocent.

One of them said that 98 per cent of the people commit a murder in the heat of the moment. He said that when the judiciary gave them punishment, it should also consider why the crime was committed or what the circumstances were. While another one said that when he committed the crime he was very young and now after 15 years he has realised that what he did was not 'correct'. Another prisoner said that he was 18 years and five days old when he was arrested and that he learned his lesson in life the hard way and he blamed the judiciary which did not consider his age while handing out the punishment. Similarly many prisoners spoke that they were guilty of what they have done but the system does not give them a chance.

Concurrently, there were prisoners who spoke about their anxiety and nervousness. A prisoner narrated a ghost story that he 'experienced' from his childhood. He claimed that the prison also had 'ghosts' because many people died in the prison. He said that while sleeping at night he felt a sense of heaviness in his chest. He felt that a sword was hanging over his head which might fall on him any time. He continued that he lay down to sleep but the tears would not stop and if he slept, he had nightmares. Another prisoner associated any kind of thread fallen from his shirt, sack, etc. with the noose. It made him nervous and he considered it '*ashub*' (bad omen) because a thread resembles a noose. One of the prisoners said that he felt restless and nervous about his daily existence and said that he has not slept soundly for the past 14 years. This prisoner also said that he stopped his reading habits and forgot every book he read before. He often saw a dream where his school teachers were present and all of them told him that he has failed but his favourite teacher told him that he will pass. Some prisoners said that they cannot do things which they could do earlier such as speaking in English or recollect certain memories.

I could not overlook some incidences where one of the prisoners was locked in his cell because he hit a prison guard the previous day and broke the guard's left hand. The co-accused of this prisoner told me that he was 'mental' and was locked in his cell. I asked the prison officer to take me to his cell. The officer said that this prisoner was mentally disturbed. I insisted on meeting him and was taken to his cell. I was asked to wait ten metres away from his cell so that he could get dressed. After a minute or two I was asked to come near the cell which was locked. He was lying down and opened his eyes slightly to see who was there at his cell. He looked lethargic and was oblivious to things happening around him. I sat down near the cell and passed the consent note to him telling him that he could contact me through his relatives if he wished to speak to me. He did not respond but gave me a smile. This prisoner did not even know that he was given a death sentence. When I enquired with the prison official if any doctor visited him, the official responded in negative.

Prisoners spoke about the loss of agency as a part of being on the death row for such a long time. One of them said, 'I have been in the prison for such a long time that I do not even know how to talk to a woman'. Others said that they felt like 'dummies locked inside a cell' or 'just a number' inside the prison on the death row. Another prisoner said, 'I am not afraid of death. I want to regain my honour; I want to live free and I want to re-possess my name on honourable terms in the society'. On the other hand, the prisoners say, 'The impending death kills me a thousand times each day. This makes me nervous and anxious'. Some of them said that they had committed the crime in the heat of the moment or under the influence of alcohol or when they were young boys and they truly regretted it. But they observed that media always reported them as 'having no remorse' for what they did. They said, 'We cannot be crying in the court or crying all the way from the police van to the court room where the media sees us. Then how can they say that we have no remorse?' Many want to return to a normal life as citizens who obey the law. Staying in prison has changed their lives forever. On the one hand, there is a belief among prisoners that one should not be afraid of death and hope to live and on the other hand the 'fear' of being killed or executed soon exists.

An opinion voiced by all prisoners was that living on the death row is a daily struggle, tortuous and oppressive. One of the prisoners said, 'I am living in a fool's paradise, being positive that God will help and we will go out. I also tell others to be positive. This is nothing but "a fool's paradise". For the time being, the paradise is good. I do not want to come out of this paradise. If I do, I will have to walk through the dark realities of life. Why not live in this fool's paradise till then?' Indeed prisoners lose their voice but at the same time, they want to remain positive. One of them said, 'I want to go back to society and work and retrieve the honour of my name' or 'I want to die outside. This will bring back my honour'. Another prisoner said that life is stubbed out without a cause while being on death row. There are also prisoners who say that they do not want to beg before the system for their lives because the system is corrupt and that they do not want to bend and bow before the system. Some call it 'fate' and say that their 'fate' led them to death penalty. Prisoners also blame their fate for being born in poverty-stricken families. One of the prisoners said, 'When fate is bad to you, what can we do? Nobody listens to us no matter what we tell. There is no justice when one is poor'. Most prisoners said that everyone has the capacity to change and they all should be given a chance to live and to prove themselves in the society.

Summary

This chapter examines the impact of the narration of the prisoners on the readers who perhaps would 'skip a beat' just like the prisoners who skipped a beat of their heart due to the seemingly incessant torture that they suffered. Scarry says that in the course of torture, the victim loses reference to the world and gradually loses his or her human voice.[68] Prisoners on death row had at some juncture temporarily lost their human voices. The trauma of the prison experience is likely to create a consequence of temporary *voicelessness*. It is possible to take a humane view with the detailed profiling of the prisoners who are on death row. By highlighting the consequence of their incarceration and death sentence on their families, the issue of death penalty does not merely get narrowed down only to the context of the prisoner on death row. It brings into its ambit others who are affected by it. The processes leading to death penalty show the slow-torture that goes on in intensifying harassment meted out the prisoners on death row. Meanwhile, the infrastructure of the prison, especially death row is a facility designed to prolong the punishment while the prisoner lives on death row. All these factors lead to the perpetuation of death row syndrome.

---

68 Scarry, Elaine. *The Body in Pain: The Making and Unmaking of the World.* New York: Oxford University Press, 1985.

Chapter 4
Voices Creating (Dis)Harmony

Dynamics of the Voices

Dag Hammarskjöld, the second Secretary-General of the United Nations said, 'The more faithfully you listen to the voices within you, the better you will hear what is sounding outside'. To present the voices of prisoners, I have to listen to the voice within me. Being aware of the subjugation and dehumanisation of any prisoner in captivity, I wanted to give the prisoners a platform to present their voice. The voice within me only wanted to be 'brave'. However, this study cultivated in me an understanding of the harsh realities of being 'brave'. While this study is about articulating the dignity of prisoners on death row and presenting the prisoner's voice, it also provides space for my own voice.

The book is abundant with the metaphors of music. Various elements of music such as 'intonation', 'articulation', 'beat' are used to present the voices of prisoners. The introductory chapter is perhaps the 'overture of an opera' which sets the tone for an extended discussion of the death penalty within an Indian context. This prelude-of-sorts presents the necessity of conducting a study of this nature by showcasing various arguments that surround the issue of death penalty. The articulation of the methodological and ethical concerns synthesise the whole gamut of the study by explaining the *why*, *who*, *when*, *where*, *which* and *how* of this research. Just like the variations and modulations that enhance finer nuances of music, the focus on ethical and methodological concerns were an absolute necessity in this study because I was conscious of the vulnerability of the prisoners on death row. It also challenged me to consider whether ethics and methods can be separated because of the reflexive nature of qualitative research. It must be emphasised here that research in any human environment, particularly in a prison is impossible without subjective feeling. As a way forward, the articulation could be of great interest to researchers interested in working in prisons Articulation in music is about (dis)connection in tone. A beat is a unit of measurement in rhythmic time. When one skips a beat on purpose or otherwise, the music could go awry or it could produce a different style of music. But 'skipping a beat' also means being frightened or surprised. The idea for this title came from the description which of one of the prisoners on death row gave me. While narrating his story, he said that his heart skipped a beat when he thought about torture. My heart too skipped several beats on various occasions, while listening to the voices of prisoners. Finally, the intonation, the articulation and the beats have created harmony or at times disharmony.

One of my thesis advisors, Christoph (Reinprecht) told me that there is no research on this planet that has not been done before. This is not the first time that a study on the experiences and perceptions of prisoners on death row has been carried out, but certainly this is the first time it has been done in India. Jackson and Christian recorded voices of prisoners on death row in Texas prisons in the 1980s.[1] I heavily relied on this book to understand more about the topic. I, too present the voices of prisoners. Jackson was asked, 'Those men you (Bruce) and Diane interviewed and filmed on death row, how can you know when they are being self-serving and how can you know what truth is in what they say?' Jackson's answer provides a foundation for my study. He says, 'There is truth of the utterance (vocal sound) itself. The vocal is a fact, a social fact, one as valid as the other'. He enquires into what is 'true' and says the stories most give of themselves and the explanation they have for themselves are always narrative and always after the fact. Just like Jackson's and Christian's study says,

> The information that you find in this book is how people on death row perceive their experience and how they present it: two sets of information, one contained within the other. You as a reader, have to decide whether the voices they offer present a real vison of that world of the condemned; you cannot argue the presentation of the self they offer, for those are no more or less authentic or fictional than any autobiography and they are facts as in any autobiography.

Likewise, this book brings out the voices of prisoners and helps in comprehending a part of their lives which must not be 'deliberately silenced' or 'preferably unheard'.

This chapter presents the (dis)harmony created by the vocals of the prisoners on death row. To aid the vocal presentation, the interpretations of the findings based on the research questions are explored. These interpretations expose the strengths and limitations of the study which throws light on areas that can become sites of further research. It would be inadequate to merely portray only the prisoners; therefore, this study encapsulates the other actors who play indispensable roles in death penalty cases. Based on the findings, there are recommendations made for the actors who influence the processes leading to the death penalty. Furthermore, the paradox of the 'rarest of rare' is an inevitable discussion that exposes the loopholes in the theory of the 'rarest of rare'.

According to the most recent Prison Statistics available from 2013, there are 382 prisoners on death row in India. When I was conducting my study in

---

1 Jackson, Bruce and Diane Christian. *Death Row*. New Brunswick, NJ: Transaction Publishers, 1980.

2011, the then available Prison statistics of 2007 indicated that there were 186 prisoners on death row. I interviewed 111 prisoners in 16 prisons from six states in India from February 2011 to August 2011. The purpose of the study was to understand the experiences and perceptions of death row prisoners in India. The specific objectives were to understand the profiles of prisoners on death row; the stages that prisoners experience before being sentenced to death and how prisoners perceived and experienced their conditions on death row. The main question was to find out if the dignity of prisoners was upheld while they confronted the criminal justice system.

Similarly prisoners on death row are not distant from the structures of prison and punishment which deprive them of their liberty. There have been many studies both in India and abroad on prisoners and their lives in prison. These studies also include the conditions of the families of prisoners, the impact of their incarceration, the children of prisoners and women prisoners. Punishment as a concept has also been dealt with in sociology, philosophy, anthropology, criminology and other sciences. The concept of dignity, a cross-cutting theme mainly used in philosophy played a major role in defining the worth of an individual after World War II. The concept of dignity has been used in the Universal Declaration of Human Rights which is referred to the intrinsic worth of a person and therefore an inherent right of an individual which cannot be taken away.

When 'dignity' is verified in the context of people deprived of liberty, it is compelling to look at what it means for prisoners on death row. There are several Indian Supreme Court judgments which look at the concept of dignity of prisoners. However this cannot be the only factor verifying the dignity of prisoners on death row. At the same time, an empirical study with prisoners on death row cannot be used as a stand-alone tool to understand the dignity of prisoners. Nevertheless, this becomes a contributing factor to understanding the meaning of dignity through the voices of prisoners themselves. Thus the statement by Justice Hosbet Suresh is relevant. He states that, 'We do not know the person whom death sentence is given except for the crime that s/he has been charged with.' We will never hear the voices of prisoners, unless we deliberately choose to listen. Therefore, they have to be given a chance to speak and to be heard.

Nevertheless it is important to mention that it is nearly impossible to explore the lives of death row prisoners in the span of a 25-minute interview. However, bringing the voices of these prisoners to the public seems imperative in the face of growing public opinion that endorses death penalty. Therefore there is a need to 'know' these men and women who are on death row. Contrary to the widely-held notion that prisoners on death row are '*dangerous*', '*hard core criminals*', '*cannot be reformed*', '*have no guilt or remorse*' – this research has foregrounded the voices of these '*dangerous criminals*' by highlighting the aspect of dignity. The findings reveal the demographic profiles of prisoners on death row; their families; the processes leading to death penalty; the infrastructure of death row; their lives on death row and the death row phenomenon. These reveal the violation or restoration of dignity while confronting the criminal justice system.

Interpreting the Findings

Although some results turned out to be predictable, there were a few unpredictable results. These results thus have an impact on the implications of the study. Four salient features have emerged in this study based on the findings. They are as follows:

Social Exclusion, Marginalisation and Poverty are Antecedents to Death Penalty

The analysis shows that death row prisoners are overwhelmingly and disproportionately male and belong to a lower socio-economic background. Most of them are academically deficient. The study reveals that most of the prisoners were arrested while they were in their twenties. They spent most of their thirties and forties in prison. Since prisoners on death row are not allowed to work, the most productive years of their lives are spent sitting idle in a prison waiting to be executed. In terms of education, more than 50 per cent of the prisoners completed their studies up to tenth grade whereas 17 per cent of the prisoners were illiterate and were not even registered in school. Some prisoners were professionally qualified and some completed their education in prison. This also means that when they were outside, they did not have jobs which paid them enough. Most of them worked as daily wage workers.

Prisoners on death row represented diverse religious, cultural and ethnic backgrounds thereby characterising the diversity of India. In India, society is ridden with class, caste and gender bias, hence it is essential to examine the above-mentioned variables in this light. Almost half of the prisoners (44 per cent) refused to identify their caste. Deliberately not providing data is 'data' in itself. Among the 56 per cent who revealed their caste identity: 37 per cent belonged to the lower castes and 19 per cent were upper castes prisoners. Lower castes are segregated socially and physically in India. They are situated in the outer boundaries of society. Though today things have changed in terms of the physical barrier, lower castes often do not have enough resources to live in the centre of the city or the village. The prisoners on death row who belong to lower castes were spatially marginalised even when they lived outside in their villages as well as in prison. These prisoners are located in the periphery of the barracks or cells which are damp and closer to the toilets.

Similarly, their religion plays a role in them being implicated especially on terrorism-related charges. It was always a Muslim that one would meet on death row in terrorism- related charges. Their languages play a role in their not being able to understand the proceedings of the case. Most of the prisoners do not speak English which is used very often in courts and in documents. This goes against them in terms of them being informed about various developments of their case. Since they have low levels of education or no education at all, they often work as daily wage workers. This does not give them a chance to have high social contacts. This further pushes them towards not receiving information on the case or access to efficient lawyers. The variables of religion, language, education, and occupation all are linked to the prisoner being marginalised and socially excluded.

When prisoners began narrating their experiences, they started with their families; even the ones who were convicted for murdering a family member talked about the surviving member(s). In most cases due to the incarceration of the breadwinner, the families left behind live in abject poverty. When a person is incarcerated, the families suffer huge financial burden. This is because of the legal expenses and expenses required for the members outside to survive. The uncertainty of their execution not only affects the prisoner in terms of the death penalty syndrome but also affects their families in diverse ways. Older parents die, partners remarry and children do not complete their education. These are not new findings on families affected by incarceration. Their incarceration further destroys the fabric of a family unit and one cannot ignore the negative financial, emotional, social and mental impact of death sentence on family members. They lose contact with the larger society and one prisoner articulated it succinctly. He said he missed out on an entire generation of family members.

The argument that prisoners are a socially-excluded and marginalised group holds water. Furthermore, it is important to note that it is this very social exclusion and marginalisation that leads them to death row. Their poverty does not allow them to hire good lawyers; their lack of knowledge of the legal system makes them stay in prison. The lack of information on their rights as prisoners and as detainees further makes them vulnerable.

The Death Penalty is a Phenomenon Constructed by State Machinery

Certain crimes are given the death penalty and these include murder, waging a war against the Government of India, treason, kidnapping for ransom, dacoity with murder and so on and so forth. This has been elaborately mentioned in the previous chapters. However based on the Bachan Singh vs the State of Punjab[2]

2 Bachan Singh v State of Punjab, 2 SCJ 474 (1980); AIR 1980 SC 898; AIR 1982 SC 1325; 1 SCR 145 (1983).

and Machhi Singh And Others vs State Of Punjab,[3] the death penalty must be given to the 'rarest of rare' which means that when a crime disturbs the 'collective conscience' of society and when it is carried out in an extremely brutal, grotesque, diabolical, revolting or dastardly manner. However, not all prisoners who have committed the above crimes are given the death penalty. The question is: which crimes enter the 'rarest of rare' category? The processes that lead to death penalty feed into the 'rarest of rare' category. It begins with the arrest which is based on 'class and/or caste', 'coercion' and 'charge'.

The findings reveal that it is the poor and the marginalised who are largely arrested. They are coerced into being arrested. They might have had a history of petty crimes but they are 'charged' with crimes which are not solved. Furthermore, the stay in the lock-up is ridden with mental, emotional and physical torture. This torture leads to them confessing whatever the police version of the crime is. The accused signs the confessional paper and this is presented as evidence in court. Even though during the trial they mention that this confessional statement was extracted under pressure, this is ignored. Their voices here are deliberately silence or unheard. The accused is taken to the doctors for a check-up; but none of the doctors write in the reports about the injury marks on their bodies which were as a result of the torture in detention.

They are taken to judicial custody after this and the trial begins. The police file a charge sheet when the trial begins and as per the law it has to be filed within 90 days of arrest. The charge sheet is basically a document which 'charges' the prisoners with crimes based on the Indian Penal Code, 1860. It has the description, evidence and circumstances of the crime. In short, the police write a 'story of the crime as it happened'. The 'production of stories' by the police in a charge sheet describes the 'gruesome' crime of the prisoners. Prisoners are forced to confess their crime in custody, they are asked to sign documents. These documents go against the prisoners because the prosecution finally nails them based on this charge sheet. This 'story' in the charge sheet finally determines whether or not the crime falls under the category of the 'rarest of rare'. The police want the accused to be nailed not because they are personal enemies, but because the system puts pressure on the police to 'solve' the case. Consequently, they go to any extent to 'solve' a case: making 'auxiliary' arrests of juveniles, pregnant women and older persons etc. Magistrates who are supposed to enquire about the prisoners' condition in the lock-up, very often do not even look at them. They are known to turn a blind eye to this cruel treatment by the police. Prisoners are tutored before they are taken before a magistrate. They are warned that they should not open their mouths but when they are allowed to speak, they are tutored on what must be said.

3 Machhi Singh And Others v State Of Punjab 1983 AIR 957, 1983 SCR (3) 413.

Even when prisoners have openly told of their torture, they were sent back to police custody. When the trial begins, generally a legal aid lawyer is provided by the government. This lawyer in most cases remains absent. They are literally the invisible contributors leading to the death penalty. Even when they are present, they hardly open their mouths to argue. Similarly, public opinion feeds into the 'collective conscience' of society. This public opinion is generated by the media. Since the media is not very independent it writes stories based on the information provided by the police officers. They read the charge sheet; they describe the crime, just as the police describe it to them. This 'story' that the police generates is a result of torture, tutoring and threatening the accused in custody. Amnesty International calls the death penalty a phenomenon where the State kills. This book reveals that 'rarest of rare' is a phenomenon produced by various actors who directly or indirectly are part of the state machinery. These actors include the police, magistrates, prosecutors, lawyers, doctors and media personnel. The nexus between these actors is undeniable and they all act as part of the state machinery. Thus, it would not be wrong to interpret that the death penalty is a phenomenon 'constructed' by the state machinery producing the concept of 'rarest of rare'.

(Non)Violation of Dignity

Upholding the dignity of the prisoner after confronting the criminal justice system was the main theme of the study. Prisoners narrated their experience and perceptions after they were arrested. This included the processes leading to death penalty and their interaction with the actors and system. Dignity is a multi-faceted concept with various components such as intrinsic worth; human rights; feeling humiliated and the feeling of being powerless. The section will discuss how data reveals how each of the components of dignity can be violated or restored. This will be discussed by looking at the processes that occur after they are arrested or when they confront the criminal justice system and by their interaction with actors and the system.

The vulnerability of prisoners' class and caste background contributes to the violation of dignity. One of the ways of interpreting their not revealing their caste-identity is that it is perhaps a mechanism to avoid exposing their vulnerability to the system (including me) since the already marginalised and socially-excluded category is mocked and verbally abused based on their class, caste, religious, educational and occupational background.

The processes leading to death penalty are: arrest, being in the lock-up, being produced in front of the magistrate for the first time; being sent to police lock-up or sent to judicial custody; judicial custody; trial and being sentenced to death. The perception of the violation of dignity occurred when prisoners were arrested and were not given a reason for their arrest. The next instance was when they were tortured in custody. The powerlessness that a person feels at the hands of the tortures takes their dignity away. They were physically and verbally abused in the lock-up. The most that prisoners talked about was the torture, threatening and tutoring that happened in the lock-up. Also terming torture as 'regular work' by both the police and the prisoners is to be questioned. The accepted norm of being tortured in custody is a result of their losing worth as a human being which results in violation of dignity. In the lock-up prisoners were not given regular food. They were given urine to drink or excrement to eat. It was a further violation of their worth as a human. Also, stripping them and electrocuting them created a terrible sense of pain and humiliation. Having access to health, family and lawyers also contributed to their dignity. When they wanted to meet their families, they were not allowed to. When they were in pain after their torture, they were not given any health care. They had no idea that they could meet a lawyer immediately or they could remain silent in custody. Remaining silent was not an option because they were tortured to 'confess' or to agree to the version of the police. Further threats to rape the female relatives of prisoners or female relatives being sexually molested by police officers contribute to the powerless of prisoners as victims.

Further, when prisoners are produced before magistrates, it was not verified whether they were tortured in custody. When magistrates asked questions, they did not check whether the prisoners repeated tutored responses. When police exercise their power to tutor prisoners to 'act' in a certain way in front of the magistrate, prisoners are reduced to becoming 'victims of the state'. This lack of empathy by the magistrates resulted in mental and emotional torture. Prisoners regard a magistrate as someone who is neutral; however, they are often disappointed in this aspect. Many narrated instances where magistrates were corrupt or had prejudices about the case based on media reports. There were three instances though, where prisoners felt their dignity was restored or upheld. Once a magistrate insisted that she wished to speak to the prisoner alone but the police informed her that he (the prisoner) is 'dangerous'. She stated, 'He must be dangerous for you, not for me'. In this instance, the prisoner felt that he was valued and not treated with prejudice. In the second instance, the prisoner banged his head in the court and asked the magistrate to intervene to find out where his wife was detained. The magistrate asked the police to immediately produce his wife in court. She was immediately produced. In the third instance, the prisoner said that he felt safer in judicial custody than in police lock-up. Had he known that in a magistrate's custody (prison), he would be safe, he would have never signed those blank confessional statements.

Another instance where prisoners felt the violation of their dignity was during the identification parade in lock-up or in the prison. They were mocked and scorned during this parade where the victim or eye-witnesses came and identified them. The officers verbally mocked and abused the prisoner which contributed to the violation of dignity.

During trial, their experiences often equated to their violation of dignity. Many of them reported being escorted like cattle to the court. They were handcuffed from morning until evening. Another instance when they felt powerless was when they did not follow the arguments or procedures in court because of their lack of understanding of the language used or the procedure itself. In one instance, the prisoner was informed about his death sentence by a court announcer (who announces the entry of the judge). Another instance of the violation of dignity is when the public prosecutor goes to the extent of humiliating the prisoners by labelling them as dangerous criminals or Muslim fundamentalists or sex maniacs. The pain was greater when the magistrate did not stop the prosecutor from labelling these prisoners. Also another instance of violation of dignity was when their own lawyers did not appear in court or when they did not argue or when the lawyers blamed the prisoners for signing confessional statements. The lack of empathy from their own lawyers pained them more.

The findings reveal that the media is an actor in the processes leading to death penalty. The trial by media is often a disadvantage to the case of the prisoner. None of them reported that media was empathetic towards them or ever reported incidences of torture even when they saw the marks of injury on them. All of them felt violated about the movies that were made about them or about the books or reports written about them. Most of them felt humiliated reading the reports which contributed to a violation of dignity. In some cases, their daily routines were reported to the media by prison officials. This pained them the most that their lives were scrutinised and reported to media who added their own 'spice' to the story. Also, another instance of the violation of dignity occurred when media reported about the families of prisoners or printed the photographs of their children. One of the other actors involved in the processes leading to the death penalty and then on death row is the doctor. Doctors have hardly reported incidences of torture when the prisoner is in the police lock-up. This contributes to the violation of their right to be not tortured. Furthermore, prison doctors violate the dignity of prisoners by asking them about their cases rather than about their illness.

Hunger strike is very peculiar to prisons. It is a means where the body is used as a weapon against the state. Carrying out a hunger strike is an instance where prisoners on death row perceived that they upheld their own dignity or the dignity of the fellow prisoner for whom the hunger strike was carried out. Prisoners have gone on hunger strike to voice their dissent or to obtain certain facilities. The use of the body as a weapon against the state by carrying out a hunger strike has existed since the freedom struggle movement (in India) and exists today in prisons across the world. Prison authorities try to dismiss this dissent or claiming of rights by threatening to kill them. They show their callousness by urging the prisoners to die of hunger. In most cases, prisoners manage to express their dissent or claim their rights. When action is taken after prisoners' have expressed dissent or claimed rights, they feel that their rights and dignity are upheld. These included being taken to the hospital when extremely sick or merging their cases together in one court rather than attending 15 court rooms or a speedy decision in their death sentence matter.

Being on death row is an extremely harrowing experience. This includes insomnia, hallucination, fear and anxiety which break the spirit of a prisoner on death row. The uncertainty of the impending death sentence creates anxiety which is called death row syndrome. This syndrome is actually a violation of the dignity of the prisoner as it amounts to living in fear each moment. Also 'not-knowing-what-happens-tomorrow' contributes to their living in fear and pain. Being humiliated and reminded about the crimes they are convicted for, by prison officials and prison visitors is a violation of their dignity. There were no aspects of death row that made them happy or upheld their dignity. Being in solitary confinement has violated as well as upheld dignity. Some prisoners like the 'privacy' while some complained of overcrowding in these single cells. Again the ones who were marginalised outside are still marginalised on death row. They are housed together in cells as there is overcrowding

The findings show that prisoners have a clear perception of the factors affecting dignity. These are being physically, verbally and mentally abused; being humiliated; inducing fear and pain; labelling and marginalising them on account of their caste and class. At the same time, they have expectations on how to maintain dignity. Prisoners have conflicting opinions about death penalty themselves. The prisoners on death row for terror -crimes are of the opinion that rapists and murderers should be hanged and vice-versa. Murderers argue that murders like the ones they have committed fetched life imprisonment for some others and they received the death penalty. While juxtaposing the death sentence and dignity, prisoners have placed dignity on a higher pedestal. Many said that they want to restore the honour that was lost. Even though prisoners talked about the uncertainty of being executed, they also said that they were not afraid of death itself. For them the most important aspect was to regain the dignity and honour that they lost in the processes leading to the death penalty. Also, they were concerned about restoring their dignity in the society that they have lived earlier. What emerges from the analysis is that prisoners wish to be respected and acknowledged as people who deserve to be treated with respect no matter what they are accused of. It is underlined how prisoners wish to be participants in the carrying out of justice even when it means that it is death that might be handed over to them. This highlights a shift from the previous perceptions of the system (court, police) taking on the expert role and the prisoners assuming the passive role as receivers of punishment. It highlights the need that prisoners have to be respected from the time they are confronted with the criminal justice system as each of them value their dignity more than the punishment (death sentence) itself.

Limitations and Strengths

There are limitations to every book and this book is no exception. The wide breadth of knowledge on death penalty has not been captured. There is a (deliberate) omission of discussion on the philosophical debate of dignity or analysis of Indian Supreme Court Judgments or empirical research related to death penalty. The scope of this book did not include any of these. The first chapter tries to provide the most recent ones to achieve a satisfactory distillation of current knowledge. One of the limitations of the study was that only current prisoners on death row were included in the study. The prisoners whose sentences were commuted to life were not included deliberately. This was because of the time constraints and because prisoners whose death sentences were commuted to life did not have the same agony as prisoners on death row. With my previous experience of researching with prisoners on death row, I have observed that life sentence prisoners have different concerns. These were finishing their sentences, going on parole or furlough. These same prisoners when they were on death row were afraid of death and could not talk about 'normal' life except for expressing their anxiety.

Even though there is a vast amount of literature that is available, there is hardly any empirical data on this topic. Hence I could not compare my findings with any research studies. There was a lack of statistical data on prisoners on death row. As mentioned earlier, there was only one empirical study in India on this subject. It was a small-scale case-study with 13 prisoners on death row in Maharashtra. Most researches in India related to prisoners on death row in India deliberate on jurisprudence and trends in execution. None of the studies discuss experiences of prisoners on death row in India. However, there have been many empirical studies in the United States; the most relevant one to this research was a study by Bruce Jackson conducted in Texas in the 1980s. There are several reports by the Ex-United Nations Special Rapporteur on Torture – Professor Dr Manfred Nowak, reports of Amnesty International and other NGOs based on primary and/or secondary data which talk about death row prisoners' conditions but not related to Indian prisoners.

These limitations also became the strength of the study. The study provides a reliable background to conduct similar studies on a large scale in India. It contributes to the debate that there are not enough studies done in India. It is also relevant because it gives voice to prisoners who are either silenced or deliberately unheard. It is important to understand who these prisoners are, how they end up on death row and how the State as a whole contributes to people ending up on death row. Methodologically, the study has its limitations and strengths. These have been elaborated, but the most important methodological limitation was grounding it in a theoretical framework that would provide adequate answers. Both phenomenology and symbolic interactionism have their own limitations in terms of empirical research, however, this approach gave enough flexibility to re-frame questions based on the situation.

Furthermore, since there were no other studies to rely upon, this methodological interpretation was considered to be the most appropriate. Additionally, this book very clearly mentions the methodological and ethical concerns which will contribute to the knowledge of prison research. It will be useful for future research done in an Indian prison setting. This study collected information directly from prisoners on death row and recorded the infrastructure of the prisons where death row prisoners are housed. The study also provides insight from the perspective of prison officials who are the custodians of death row prisoners. In addition to all these, there was also plenty of information collected from the families of prisoners. The interviews were conducted in the language that the prisoners spoke. Translators were called upon when required and this allowed for the inclusion of many prisoners. This book is also significant because there is a strong feeling concerning death penalty in India, as expressed by the Supreme Court. It says that western experiences and arguments based on western statistical studies are not necessarily relevant to the social conditions and educational level of India. Hence, the data used in western studies cannot be compared to the Indian situation especially in the case of abolishing death penalty.[4]

Future Research

Given the limited research to date on death row prisoners in India, there are many areas where further investigation is recommended. An empirical study using a larger sample of prisoners on death row could be conducted. For instance, into the link between media reports and the death penalty, or into how public opinion shapes the collective conscience of the society. Viable research is possible in analysing the roles of various actors involved in the processes leading to death penalty. Probable areas of research could include the death penalty and doctors; death penalty and police officers; the death penalty and magistrates and the death penalty and legal aid lawyers. Also, it is essential to study women on death row. As it is there is almost no research on women prisoners and even

4 Hood, Roger and Carolyn Hoyle. *The Death Penalty: A Worldwide Perspective.* Oxford: Oxford University Press, 2014.

fewer on women prisoners on death row. Another research possibility is an empirical study with prisoners whose sentences have been commuted to life from death. A comparative study on the difference in being a prisoner for life and a prisoner on death row would fill the gaps left in literature around the aforementioned area. The controversy regarding death penalty has not been informed by research directed towards death row prisoners. The scarcity of research with prisoners on death row is frightening. Empirical research with this population could benefit correctional, judicial and public policy.

Implications and Recommendations

To identify the implications of the interpretations based on the findings, it is imperative to discuss this in relation to the various actors and the institutions that are involved in awarding the death penalty. These actors and institutions intersect.

The actors in this study are the police, magistrates, lawyers, doctors and media. Each of them has a role to play which can lead to upholding the dignity of prisoners. First it is important to deal with police as a system. Since they exercise the most form of raw power within the whole criminal justice system, it is essential that they are sensitised to human rights concerns. This should begin with their education and training. Also, the curriculum should do away with outdated theories such as Lombroso Theory or teach that with a critical perspective. Similarly, the training curriculum of police officers should have a strong human rights component. Apart from this, police officers from all ranks should be made responsible and accountable not to violate the power that they have.

Secondly, the accused are supposed to be produced within twenty-four hours of their arrest in front of the magistrate. However, that is far from what happens in reality in most cases. Prisoners described their stay in lock-up or other places of detention (for days or months on end) and the torture they faced with immense pain and shame. The D.K. Basu Guidelines requires enquiring about the treatment of individuals in custody. But hardly has any magistrate enquired or sent the prisoner immediately to her/his (judicial or magisterial) custody. This custody is basically prison, thus the very protectors become (indirect) perpetrators of torture. The police officer concerned can be prosecuted the same day if the D. K. Basu Guidelines are applied. Also, magistrates need to proactively enquire the age of individuals who seem to be juveniles. The practice of taking detainees to the magistrate's home should be stopped as this leads to further violation of the rights of the individual in detention.

Thirdly the lawyers – both defence and prosecutors highlight the need for higher responsibility. It is very important to have adequate legal representation during trial stage but it is equally important to have lawyers dedicated to work for prisoners who are sentenced to death. Not many lawyers work on this or the ones that work are not competent enough. This indicates that there should be training for lawyers and prosecutors regarding capital punishment cases. There could also be a heavy component of human rights in the curriculum of law education.

Fourth, doctors are important actors in this whole process. They are the ones to be first in contact with the prisoner after they face heavy torture. It is therefore disturbing to hear from prisoners that many of them were given a 'normal' certificate after their medical examination even when there were clear injury marks on them. But the dilemma the doctors face is: Who could they report these incidences of torture to? Registering a complaint in the same police station where the accused is tortured is not a good solution. Hence, there should be a (reporting) system where torture can be reported to the magistrates directly. For instance when the prisoner is taken to a civil hospital, a sealed report could be sent to the Magistrates of the particular jurisdiction. This report could indicate whether the prisoner faced torture in custody or not. Also when the accused is transferred from police custody to judicial custody, it is important to report any case of torture that must have occurred in police custody. Similarly prison doctors call posting in the prison as 'punishment' transfer. This attitude needs a change.

Finally, another actor is the media. The media, though it should be independent, has often reported stories from the state side. Prisoners have often responded how their cases were tried by media and how this has affected their case. One of my lawyer friends shared that a TV serial was made on a defendant he was representing. The judge said in the court room that 'But this was not how it was shown on TV'. Creating a bias is certainly not the job of media. It should ideally present both sides of the story in the news. However, in cases of prisoners, only one side of the story is presented.

Similarly, there are two institutions that are relevant to the debate on the death penalty. The courts play an important role as an institution when an accused is tried. First, given the interpretation that poverty is an antecedent to death penalty, it would be imperative for the court to look at the socio-economic background of the prisoners before handing out the death penalty. The significantly large proportion of poor prisoners on death row is disturbing and reveals a system which excludes and marginalises prisoners. Hence, there should be a more intensive evaluation within the criminal justice system to ascertain the social and economic identity of prisoners who are awarded the death penalty. This speaks to the need for more research on the lives and background of prisoners. There also needs to be an assessment on the available literature and the will to reduce these gaps. Also, the courts should consider if the accused was represented by a lawyer regularly, if the prisoner is an adult, if s/he claims innocence and proactively enquire if any torture occurred. It is dangerous to accept torture in custody as 'regular work' or 'normal'. Prisoners should be informed about their rights, the reason for their arrest and provided legal aid when they cannot afford a private lawyer. Even though these exist on paper, only a court can verify this. Courts have to see beyond what the prisoner is 'tutored' to speak in the court.

The second institution that plays a major role is the government structure such as prisons, Ministry of Home Affairs and Ministry of Law and Justice which contributes to the functioning of a democracy. It would be relevant to inform oneself before policy decisions and laws are made. For this the most important would be encouraging more research in the criminal justice sector. The debate on the death penalty in India is not informed by any research conducted in India. It is very much western and this has been criticised by policy makers. This hinders any decision that legislative members can take regarding abolition or retention of death penalty. Hence, it would be important to encourage researches in the criminal justice system as a whole and especially on the issue of death penalty. Also in prison research, instead of looking at researchers as instruments to improve the system, they are often perceived as a threat to the system.

Paradox of the 'Rarest of Rare'

The voices of prisoners underscore the importance of maintaining a focus on dignity in the criminal justice system. The voices show that prisoners experience this violation of dignity right from the time they are arrested till the time they are on death row. Prisoners are also given death sentence because the judiciary thinks that the person is incapable of reform and since the person will die 'soon', there is also no need to try for reformation or rehabilitation. The whole purpose of prison collapses as its main goal is the rehabilitation and reformation of prisoners.

But the question is how the doctrine of 'rarest of rare' interferes with the concept of dignity. Is it the death penalty or the processes that lead to it that most violate the dignity of prisoners? There is a vast amount of literature on this doctrine of the 'rarest of rare' which has been discussed in the previous chapters. However, with the above interpretation of the findings, it is revealed that poverty, social exclusion and marginalisation are antecedents to death penalty; that death penalty is a state-constructed machinery and after confronting the criminal justice system, the dignity of the prisoners is not upheld. The doctrine of the 'rarest of rare' fetches prisoners the death penalty.

To me this doctrine seems to be dangerously twisted. How can one crime be rare and the other not? How is it that one murder disturbs the collective conscience but a similar one does not even trigger a discussion? How is it that Nirbhaya's rape and murder invokes mass protests but Soni Sori's case or Khairlanji rape and murder do not disturb our consciences? Our conscience should be disturbed when a woman is molested in the bus and not only when stones or sticks are shoved into her. Our conscience should be disturbed when a woman is considered an accused for being raped. Our conscience should be disturbed when Suzette Jordan was not allowed to enter a restaurant because she was a 'rape victim'. Our conscience should be disturbed when a man is killed on a street and not only when his head and body is cut into tiny parts. Our conscience should not only be disturbed when a middle-class woman working in a five start hotel is killed on account of a terror attack but also when a female foetus is aborted. The rarest of rare crime is a concept which has been manipulated in the court and left for interpretation by the judges. A murder is a murder. A life is lost. One life is as important as the other. It is equally contradictory when one murder is handed death penalty and the other life imprisonment.

But what is the purpose of understanding the concept of the dignity of prisoners who are sentenced to death? They are after all prisoners convicted for some gruesome murder which falls under the category of 'rarest of rare crimes' and which disturbs the conscience of the society. Even when the state executes, it is murder. Executing a person so that rapes and murders will decrease may perhaps never happen as long as humanity exists. The argument that death penalty would act as a deterrent also fails because if that was the case, then the incidence of rape and murder should have decreased from 2004 onwards after Dhanojoy Chatterjee was executed. Deterrence in terms of terrorist attacks is not going to happen because of the execution of Kasab and Guru. Mahatma Gandhi was killed, his executors hanged, Indira Gandhi was killed, her executors were hanged. This did not stop people from conspiring to kill Rajiv Gandhi. Killing Kasab did not prevent any further terror attacks. By no means is it suggested that people who violate others' right to live should be left free. Nirbhayas, Soni Sori, Suzette Jordan, the family of Khairlanji and all the others whose precious lives were taken or rights violated must receive justice. The only question we need to raise is if death penalty based on whatever reasons is an answer to this? An eye for an eye will indeed make the whole world blind. The majority cannot decide what is best for the minority. Hence, the so-called collective conscience of a society which is largely gender and caste-biased cannot be the criteria for handing out the death penalty.

Appendix

INTERVIEW GUIDE FOR PRISONERS ON DEATH ROW

(February 2011 – August 2011)

Profile of the prisoner

Name
Age
Gender
Religion
Language
Ethnic background
Education
Occupation
Present stage of appeal
Family members and relation with prisoners after incarceration

Arrest

Date of arrest
Whom did you inform (as third party) about the arrest?
What were the reasons given for your arrest?
Could you share your experience or perceptions during arrest?
Could you share your experience or perceptions while appearing before the magistrate?

Interrogation

How and where did the interrogation take place?
What were your experiences when you were taken to the crime-scene?
What happened during the identification parade (if there was one)?
How many times did you have access to relatives, doctors and lawyers and what were your experiences with them?
Were you asked to sign blank documents?

Judicial custody (prison)

How long did the trial last?
How were you housed in judicial custody (Solitary confinement or barracks) and what were your experiences or perception during this period?
How often were you taken to the court and what were your experiences while being taken to court?
What are the facilities that you get as an undertrial?
How was the behaviour of other prisoners towards you?
Could you share experiences or perceptions with regards to prison officials or prison visitors or doctors?

Court room experience

How difficult or how easy was it understand the court proceedings?
What were your experiences or perceptions with magistrates and lawyers?
When did the prosecution demand the death sentence and what were your perceptions or experiences about it?
When was the first time the death sentence was demanded?
Did you expect a death sentence in your case? Why?

Media

What were your experiences or perception of the media?
How did the family respond to the news articles or news on television about you?
What version of the story was in the media?
What were your experiences with journalists?
Were there any positive write-ups about you? Example: you finishing education in prison?

Life on death row

Period on death row
After how many days of your conviction, were you brought to the security yard?
Could you describe the experience of being brought to death row?
What were the rules that you had to follow?
What are the facilities that you get on death row?
What kind of information did you have about the conditions on death row or about death row? What is your daily routine?
What are the conditions of the cell you are housed in?
How often do you have access to your lawyers, doctors and relatives?

Who are the other visitors on death row and what are your experiences with them?
What does it mean to be in death cell?
What are the more difficult things and less difficult things being on death row?
Is there any easy aspect of being on death row?

References

Books

Abu-Jamal, Mumia. *Live from Death Row*. New York: Harper Perennial, 1996.

Arditti, Joyce A., Jennifer Lambert-Shute and Karen Joest. 'Saturday morning at the jail: Implications of incarceration for families and children'. *Family Relations* 52, no. 3 (2004): 195–204.

Babcock, Philip. *Webster's Third New International Dictionary*. Springfield, IL: G & C Merriam Company, 1971.

Baker, Cynthia, Judith Wuest and Phyllis Noerager Stern. 'Method slurring: The grounded theory/phenomenology example'. *Journal of Advanced Nursing* 17, no. 11 (2006): 1355–60.

Balagopal, K. 'Of capital and other punishments'. *Economic and Political Weekly* 33, no. 38 (1998): 2438–47.

Batra, Bikramjeet. 'Don't be cruel ... : The "death row phenomenon" and India's "delay" jurisprudence', in Hood, Roger and Surya Deva, eds. *Confronting Capital Punishment in Asia: Human Rights, Politics and Public Opinion*. Oxford: Oxford University Press, 2013, pp. 287–312.

Bentham, Jeremy. *An Introduction to the Principles of Morals and Legislation (Collected Works of Jeremy Bentham)*. Oxford: Clarendon Press, 1996.

Benvenisti, Meron. *Abu Ghraib: The Politics of Torture*. Berkeley, CA: North Atlantic Books, 2004.

Beyleveld, Deryck and Roger Brownsword. *Human Dignity in Bioethics and Biolaw*. Oxford: Oxford University Press, 2001.

Bindal, Amit. and Raj C. Kumar. 'Abolition of the death penalty in India: Legal, constitutional and human rights dimension', in Hood, Roger and Surya Deva, eds. *Confronting Capital Punishment in Asia: Human Rights, Politics and Public Opinion*. Oxford: Oxford University Press, 2013, pp. 123–40.

Black, Henry Campbell. *Black's Law Dictionary*. St. Paul: West Publishing Company, 1957.

Blank, Stephen. 'Killing time: The process of waiving appeal – The Michael Ross death penalty cases'. *Journal of Law & Policy* 14 (2006): 735–77.

Bluestone, Harvey and L. Carl McGahee. 'Reaction to extreme stress: Impending death by execution'. *The American Journal of Psychiatry* 119, no. 5 (1962): 393–6.

Blumer, Herbert. *Symbolic Interactionism: Perspective and Method*. Berkeley: University of California Press, 1986.

Bogdan, Robert C. and Sari Knopp Biklen. *Qualitative Research in Education. An Introduction to Theory and Methods*. Boston, MA: Allyn & Bacon, 1998.

Bosworth, Mary, Debi Campbell, Bonita Demby, Seth M. Ferranti and Michael Santos. 'Doing prison research: Views from inside'. *Qualitative Inquiry* 11, no. 2 (2005): 249–64.

Briggs, Charles L. *Learning How to Ask: A Sociolinguistic Appraisal of the Role of the Interview in Social Science Research*. 1st edn. Cambridge: Cambridge University Press, 1986.

Camus, Albert. *Reflections on the Guillotine*. Indiana: Fridtjof-Karla Publications, 1960.

Carroll, Jenny E. 'Images of women and capital sentencing among female offenders: Exploring the outer limits of the Eighth Amendment and articulated theories of justice'. *Texas Law Review* 75 (1996): 1413–52.

Colvin, Mark. *Penitentiaries, Reformatories and Chain Gangs: Social Theory and the History of Punishment in Nineteenth-Century America*. New York: St. Martin's Press, 1997.

Cover, Robert M. *Narrative, Violence and the Law: The Essays of Robert Cover*. Edited by Martha Minow. Ann Arbor: University of Michigan Press, 1995.

Coyle, Andrew. *Understanding Prisons*. Maidenhead: Open University Press, 2005.

Creswell, John W. 'Five qualitative traditions of inquiry', in *Qualitative Inquiry and Research Design: Choosing among Five Traditions*. Thousand Oaks, CA, and London: Sage, 1998, pp. 47–72.

Cunningham, Mark D. and Mark P. Vigen. 'Death row inmate characteristics, adjustment and confinement: A critical review of the literature'. *Behavioural Sciences & the Law* 20, no. 1–2 (2002): 191–210.

Davis, Angela Y. *Are Prisons Obsolete?*. New York: Seven Stories Press, 2003.

De Vos, A.S. 'Scientific theory and professional research', in De Vos, A.S., et al. *Research at Grass Roots: For the Social Sciences and Human Service Professions*'. Pretoria: Van Schaik Publishers, 2005, pp. 27–43.

De Vos, A.S., Herman Strydom, Christa B. Fouché and C.S.L. Delport. *Research at Grass Roots: For the Social Sciences and Human Service Professions*'. Pretoria: Van Schaik Publishers, 2005.

Denzin, Norman K. *Interpretive Interactionism*. Newbury Park: Sage, 2001.

Denzin, Norman K. 'Symbolic interactionism', in Flick, Uwe et al. *A Companion to Qualitative Research*. London: Sage, 2004, pp. 81–7.

Deva, Surya 'Death penalty in the "rarest of rare" cases: A critique of judicial choice-making', in Hood, Roger and Surya Deva, eds. *Confronting Capital Punishment in Asia: Human Rights, Politics and Public Opinion*. Oxford: Oxford University Press, 2013, pp. 238–86.

Devereux, George and Weston La Barre. *From Anxiety to Method in the Behavioural Sciences*. New Babylon: Studies in Behavioral Sciences 3. The Hague: Mouton, 1967.

Dillon, Robin S. 'Self-respect: Moral, emotional, political'. *Ethics* 107, no. 2 (1997): 226–49.

Duff, R. Antony and David Garland, eds. *A Reader on Punishment.* Oxford: Oxford University Press, 1995.

Durkheim, Emile. *The Division of Labor in Society*. Trans. G. Simpson. New York: Macmillan, 1993.

Dworkin, Ronald. *Taking Rights Seriously*. Cambridge, MA: Harvard University Press, 1978.

Eckert, Julia. 'Death and the nation: State killing in India', in Sarat, Austin and Christian Boulanger, eds. *The Cultural Lives of Capital Punishment: Comparative Perspectives*. Redwood City, CA: Stanford University Press, 2005, 195–218.

Foucault, Michel. *Discipline and Punish: The Birth of the Prison.* New York: Vintage, 1977.

Freitag, Sandria B. 'Crime in the social order of colonial north India'. *Modern Asian Studies* 25, no. 2 (1991): 227–61.

Gallemore, Johnnie L., H. James Panton and Edward Kaufman. 'Inmate responses to lengthy death row confinement'. *The American Journal of Psychiatry* 129, no. 2 (1972): 167–72.

Garland, David. *The Culture of Control: Crime and Social Order in Contemporary Society*. Chicago, IL: University of Chicago Press. 2001.

Garland, David. *Peculiar Institution: America's Death Penalty in an Age of Abolition.* Boston, MA: Harvard University Press, 2010.

Garland, David. *Punishment and Modern Society: A Study in Social Theory*. Chicago, IL: University of Chicago Press, 1993.

Garland, David. 'Sociological perspectives on punishment'. *Crime and Justice* 14 (1991): 115–65.

George, Reena Mary. 'Death penalty: A human rights perspective'. University of Mumbai, 2009 (unpublished Master's Thesis).

Gewirth, Alan. 'Human dignity as the basis of rights'. in Meyer, Michael J. and William Allan Parent, eds. *The Constitution of Rights: Human Dignity and American Values*. Ithaca, NY: Cornell University Press, 1992, pp. 10–46.

Ghormode, Vijay *Death Sentence: A Struggle for Abolition.* Pune: Hind Law Publications, 2008.

Ghosh, Srikanta. *Torture and Rape in Police Custody: An Analysis*. Delhi: Ashish Publishing House, 1993.

Gifis, Steven H. *Barron's Law Dictionary*. Hauppauge, NY: Barron's Educational Series, Inc., 2010.

Gilbert, Nigel, ed. *Researching Social Life*. London: Sage, 2008.

Gilbert, Paul. 'The evolution of social attractiveness and its role in shame, humiliation, guilt and therapy'. *British Journal of Medical Psychology* 70, no. 2 (2011): 113–47.

Glaser, Barney G. and Anselm L. Strauss. *The Discovery of Grounded Theory: Strategies for Qualitative Research.* New York Aldine de Gruyter, 1967.

Goffman, Erving. 'On the characteristics of total institutions', in Walter Reed Army Institute of Research: *Symposium on preventive and social psychiatry.* Washington, DC: U.S. Government Printing Office, 1957, pp. 43–84.

Gould, Stephen Jay. *The Mismeasure of Man.* New York: Norton, 1996.

Hacking, Ian. 'Between Michel Foucault and Erving Goffman: Between discourse in the abstract and face-to-face interaction'. *Economy and Society* 33, no. 3 (2004): 277–302.

Halbar, B.G. *Lamani economy and society in change: Socio-cultural Aspects of Economic Change Among the Lamani of North Karnataka.* Delhi: Mittal Publication, 1986.

Harris, Scott R. 'What can interactionism contribute to the study of inequality? The case of marriage and beyond'. *Symbolic Interaction* 24, no. 4 (2001): 455–80.

Harrison, Selig S. and Karl Wolfgang Deutsch. *The Most Dangerous Decades: An Introduction to the Comparative Study of Language Policy in Multi-Lingual States.* Language and Communication Research Center. New York: Columbia University, 1957.

Heylin, Greg. 'Evaluating Prisons, Prisoners and Others'. *Studies in Public Policy* 6 (2001): 1–128.

Hodgkinson, Peter, ed. *Capital Punishment: New Perspectives.* Farnham: Ashgate Publishing, 2013.

Hodgkinson, Peter and William Schabas, eds. *Capital Punishment: Strategies for Abolition.* Cambridge: Cambridge University Press, 2004.

Holland, Nancy. 'Death row conditions: Progression toward constitutional protections'. *Akron Law Review* 19 (1985): 293–310.

Hood, Roger and Surya Deva, eds. *Confronting Capital Punishment in Asia: Human Rights, Politics and Public Opinion.* Oxford: Oxford University Press, 2013.

Hood, Roger and Carolyn Hoyle. *The Death Penalty: A Worldwide Perspective.* Oxford: Oxford University Press, 2014.

Hudson, Patrick. 'Does the death row phenomenon violate a prisoner's human rights under international law?'. *European Journal of International Law* 11, no. 4 (2000): 833–56.

Huggins, Martha K. and Marie-Louise Glebbeek. 'Women studying violent male institutions: Cross-gendered dynamics in police research on secrecy and danger'. *Theoretical Criminology* 7, no. 3 (2003): 363–87.

Hunt, Lynn. *Inventing Human Rights: A History.* New York and London: Norton, 2007.

Hussain, Abdul H. and Seymour Tozman. 'Psychiatry on death row'. *Journal of Clinical Psychiatry* 39, no. 3 (1978): 183–8.

Ignatieff, Michael. *A Just Measure of Pain: The Penitentiary in the Industrial Revolution.* London: Macmillan, 1978.

Irwin, John and Barbara Owen. 'Harm and the contemporary prison', in Liebling, Alison and Shadd Maruna, eds. *The Effects of Imprisonment.* Cullompton: Willan, 2005, pp. 94–117.

Jackson, Bruce. *Fieldwork.* Urbana: University of Illinois Press, 1987.

Jackson, Bruce and Diane Christian. *Death Row.* New Brunswick, NJ: Transaction Publishers, 1980.

Jacobsen, Karen and Landau, B, Loren. 'The dual imperative in refugee research: some methodological and ethical considerations in social science research on forced migration'. *Disasters* 27, no. 3 (2003): 185–206.

Johnson, David T. and Franklin E. Zimring. *The Next Frontier: National Development, Political Change and the Death Penalty in Asia.* Oxford: Oxford University Press, 2009.

Johnson, Robert. 'Under sentence of death: The psychology of death row confinement'. *Law & Psychology Review* 5 (1979): 141–92.

Jois, Mandagadde Rama. *Legal and Constitutional History of India.* Vol. 1. Delhi: Universal Law Publishing, 1984.

Kandelia, Seema and Peter Hodgkinson. 'The greater stigma? Family visits to the condemned', in Hodgkinson, Peter, ed. *Capital Punishment: New Perspectives.* Farnham: Ashgate Publishing, 2013, pp. 127–44.

Kateb, George. *Human Dignity.* Cambridge, MA: Harvard University Press, 2011.

Kaufmann, Paulus, Hannes Kuch, Christian Neuhaeuser and Elaine Webster, eds. *Humiliation, Degradation, Dehumanization: Human Dignity Violated.* Library of Ethics and Applied Philosophy, Vol. 24. Dordrecht: Springer, 2010.

Kennedy, Randall. 'Race, law and suspicion: Using color as a proxy for dangerousness', in *Race, Crime and the Law.* New York: Pantheon, 1997, pp. 136–67.

King, Anthony E. 'The impact of incarceration on African American families: Implications for practice'. *Families in Society* 74, no. 3 (1993): 145–53.

King, Roy D. 'The rise and rise of Supermax: An American solution in search of a problem?' *Punishment & Society* 1, no. 2 (1999): 163–86.

Knowles, Helen J. 'A dialogue on death penalty dignity'. *Criminology and Criminal Justice* 11, no. 2 (2011): 115–28.

Kusenbach, Margarethe. 'Street phenomenology the go-along as ethnographic research tool'. *Ethnography* 4, no. 3 (2003): 455–85.

Laitin, David D. 'Language policy and political strategy in India'. *Policy Sciences* 22, no. 3 (1989): 415–36.

Law Commission of India: 187th Report on 'Mode of Execution of Death Sentence and Incidental Matters', October 2003.

Liebling, Alison. 'Doing research in prison: breaking the silence?' *Theoretical Criminology* 3, no. 2 (1999): 147–73.

Lo, Bernard. *Resolving Ethical Dilemmas: A Guide for Clinicians.* Philadelphia, PA: Lippincott Williams & Wilkins, 2009.

Loeb, Robert H. and George F. Cole. *Crime and Capital Punishment.* New York: F. Watts, 1986.

Lofland, John. *Analyzing Social Settings: A Guide to Qualitative Observation and Analysis.* Belmont, CA: Wadsworth, 1971.

Luban, David. 'Human dignity, humiliation and torture'. *Kennedy Institute of Ethics Journal* 19, no. 3 (2009): 211–30.

Luckmann, Thomas. 'Philosophy, science and everyday life'. *Phenomenology and the Social Sciences.* 1 (1973): 143–86.

Lyons, Lewis. *The History of Punishment.* London: Amber Books, 2003.

Margalit, Avishai. *The Decent Society.* Cambridge, MA: Harvard University Press, 1996.

Martin, R. 'Community perceptions about prison construction: Why not in my backyard'? *The Prison Journal* 80, no. 3 (2000): 265–94.

Mello, Michael. 'Facing death alone: The post-conviction attorney crisis on death row'. *American University Law Review* 37 (1987): 513–607.

Mines, Diane P. *Caste in India.* Ann Arbor: Association for Asian Studies, 2009.

Mouat, Frederic John. 'On prison statistics and discipline in lower Bengal'. *Journal of the Statistical Society of London* 25, no. 2 (1862): 175–218.

Natanson, Maurice. *Phenomenology and the Social Sciences.* Vol. 1. Evanston, IL: Northwestern University Press, 1973.

Nowak, Manfred. Foreword in Kaufmann, Paulus et al., eds. *Humiliation, Degradation, Dehumanization: Human Dignity Violated.* Library of Ethics and Applied Philosophy, Vol. 24. Dordrecht: Springer, 2010: v–vi.

Nowak, Manfred. 'What practices constitute torture? US and UN standards'. *Human Rights Quarterly* 28, no. 4 (2006): 809–41.

Popper, Frank J. *Siting LULUs.* Emmitsburg: National Emergency Training Center, 1981.

Pratt, John. *Governing the Dangerous: Dangerousness, Law and Social Change.* Sydney: Federation Press, 1997.

Radelet, Michael. *Facing the Death Penalty: Essays on a Cruel and Unusual Punishment.* Philadelphia: Temple University Press, 1990.

Rubin, Herbert J. and Irene S. Rubin. *Qualitative Interviewing: The Art of Learning Data.* Thousand Oaks, CA: Sage Publications, 1995.

Sarat, Austin and Christian Boulanger, eds. *The Cultural Lives of Capital Punishment: Comparative Perspectives.* Stanford, CA: Stanford University Press, 2005.

Sartre, Jean-Paul. 1958. Preface in Alleg, Henri. *The Question.* Bison Books, 2006.

Scarry, Elaine. *The Body in Pain: The Making and Unmaking of the World.* New York: Oxford University Press, 1985.

Schabas, William. *The Abolition of the Death Penalty in International Law.* Cambridge: Cambridge University Press, 2002.

Schabas, William. *The Death Penalty as Cruel Treatment and Torture: Capital Punishment Challenged in the World's Courts*. Boston, MA: Northeastern University Press, 1996.

Schabas, William. 'Developments in criminal law and criminal justice: Execution delayed, execution denied'. *Criminal Law Forum* 5 (1994): 180–788.

Schechner, Richard and Mady Schuman, eds. *Ritual, Play and Performance: Readings in the Social Sciences/Theatre*. New York: Seabury Press, 1976.

Scheper-Hughes, Nancy. 'The primacy of the ethical: Propositions for a militant anthropology'. *Current Anthropology* 36, no. 3 (1995): 409–40.

Scherdin, Lill, ed. *Capital Punishment: A Hazard to a Sustainable Criminal Justice System?* Farnham: Ashgate Publishing, 2014.

Scott, Charles L., ed. *Handbook of Correctional Mental Health*. Washington, DC: American Psychiatric Publishing, 2009.

Shankardass, Rani Dhavan. *Punishment and the Prison: Indian and International Perspectives*. New Delhi: Sage, 2000.

Sharp, Susan F. *Hidden Victims: The Effects of the Death Penalty on Families of the Accused*. New Brunswick, NJ: Rutgers University Press, 2005.

Silverman, David. *Interpreting Qualitative Data: Strategies for Analyzing Talk, Text and Interaction* London: Sage Publications Limited, 1993.

Singh, Hira. 'Prison administration in India: Contemporary issues', in Shankardass, Rani Dhavan, ed. *Punishment and the Prison. Indian and International Perspectives*. New Delhi: Sage, 2000, pp. 112–22.

Singh, Kumar Suresh. *People of India: Maharashtra*. Vol. 30. Mumbai: Popular Prakashan, 2004.

Statman, Daniel. 'Humiliation, dignity and self-respect'. *Philosophical Psychology* 13, no. 4 (2000): 523–40.

Steinke, Ines, Ernst von Kardoff and Uwe Flick, eds. *A Companion to Qualitative Research*: London: Sage Publications Limited, 2004.

Strafer, G. Richard. 'Volunteering for execution: Competency, voluntariness and the propriety of third party intervention'. *Journal of Criminal Law and Criminology* 74 (1983): 860–912.

Strauss, Anselm and Juliet Corbin. *Basics of Qualitative Research. Techniques and Procedures for Developing Grounded Theory*. London: Sage, 1998.

Suchman, Lucy and Brigitte Jordan. 'Interactional troubles in face-to-face survey interviews'. *Journal of the American Statistical Association* 85, no. 409 (1990): 232–41.

Sykes, Gresham M. *The Society of Captives: A Study of a Maximum Security Prison*. Princeton: Princeton University Press, 1958.

Tata Institute of Social Sciences. *Forced Separation: Children of Imprisoned Mothers (An Exploration in Two Indian Cities)*, Mumbai: Prayas Publications, 2002.

Tesch, Renata. *Qualitative Research: Analysis Types and Software Tools*. New York: Falmer Press, 1990.

Travis, Jeremy. 'Invisible punishment: An instrument of social exclusion', in Mauer, Marc and Meda Chesney-Lind, eds. *Invisible Punishment: The Collateral Consequences of Mass Imprisonment*. New York: The New Press, 2002, pp. 15–36.

Unnithan, N. Prabha, ed. *Crime and Justice in India*. New Delhi: SAGE Publications India, 2013.

Valle, Ron, ed. *Phenomenological Inquiry in Psychology: Existential and Transpersonal Dimensions*. New York: Springer, 1998.

Von Eckartsberg, Rolf. 'Introducing existential-phenomenological psychology', in: Valle, Ron, ed. *Phenomenological Inquiry in Psychology: Existential and Transpersonal Dimensions*. New York: Springer, 1998, pp. 3–20.

Wacquant, Loïc. 'Deadly symbiosis when ghetto and prison meet and mesh'. *Punishment & Society* 3, no. 1 (2001): 95–133.

Wacquant, Loïc. 'The new "peculiar institution": On the prison as surrogate ghetto'. *Theoretical Criminology* 4, no. 3 (2000): 377–89.

Wax, Rosalie H. 'Reciprocity in field work', in Adams, Richard N. and Jack J. Preiss, eds. *Human Organization Research*. Homewood, IL: Dorsey, 1960, pp. 90–98.

West, Louis Jolyon. 'Psychiatric reflections on the death penalty'. *American Journal of Orthopsychiatry* 45, no. 4 (1975): 689–700.

Western, Bruce and Sara McLanahan. 'Fathers behind bars: The impact of incarceration on family formation'. *Contemporary Perspectives in Family Research* 2 (2000): 309–24.

Whitman, James Q. 'The two western cultures of privacy: Dignity versus liberty'. *Yale Law Journal* 113 (2003): 1151–221.

Wilcox, Norma and Steele, Tracey. 'Just the facts: A descriptive analysis of inmate attitudes toward capital punishment'. *The Prison Journal* 83, no. 4 (2003): 464–82.

Indian Laws Cited

Andhra Pradesh Control of Organised Crime Act, 2001 (Article 3)
Armed Forces (Special Powers) Act, 1958
Criminal Law (Amendment) Act, 2013 (Section 9)
Criminal Tribes Act, 1871
Explosive Substances (Amendment) Act, 2001(Section 3)
Habitual Offenders Act, 1952
Indian Evidence Act, 1872 (Section 24, 25, 26, 27)
Indian Penal Code, 1860 (Section 54, 73, 74, 121, 132, 194, 302, 303, 305, 307, 330, 331, 364(a), 396, 432, 433)
Indian Prevention of Atrocities Act, 1989 (Section 3 (2)(i))
Indo-Tibetan Border Police Force Act, 1992 (Section 16, 19, 20)

Jail Manual of Punjab and Haryana, ______ (Chapter XXXI, Para 847 (1) and (2))
Juvenile Justice (Care and Protection of Children) Act, 2000
Karnataka Control of Organised Crime Act, 2000 (Article 3)
Maharashtra Control of Organised Crime Act, 1999 (Article 3)
Maharashtra Prison Manual, 1978 (Chapter 'Prisoners sentenced to death')
Narcotics Drugs and Psychotropic Substances Act of India, 1985 (Article 31A).
Prevention of Terrorism Act of India, 2002 (Article 3(2)(a))
Prisons Act, 1894 (Section 30 (2))
Terrorist and Disruptive Activities (Prevention) Act of India, 1993 (Article 3, 28, 43)
The Air Force Act of India, 1950 (Section 34, 37, 38, 46)
The Code of Criminal Procedure, 1898 (Section 368(1))
The Code of Criminal Procedure, 1973 (Section 167, 354)
The Commission of Sati (Prevention) Act, 1987 (Article 4)
The Constitution of India, 2007 (Article 14, 19, 21, 51, 72)
The Unlawful Activities (Prevention) Amendment Ordinance, 2004 (Article 6)
Universal Declaration of Human Rights, 1948 (Articles 21 and 23)

Cases Cited

Bachan Singh v State of Punjab, 2 SCJ 474 (1980); AIR 1980 SC 898; AIR 1982 SC 1325; 1 SCR 145 (1983)
Bariyar v State of Maharashtra 6 S.C.C. 498 (2009)
Bhuvan Mohan Patnaik v State of Andhra Pradesh, 2 SCR 24: AIR 1974 SC 2092 (1975)
Citizen For Democracy Through Its … v State Of Assam And Others AIR 1996 SC 2193, 1996 CriLJ 3247, (1996) 1 GLR 682 (1995)
D. K. Basu v State of West Bengal – AIR (SC)-610, 1997-SCC-1-416.
Dhananjoy Chatterjee Alias Dhana v State Of West Bengal, 2004 All MR (Cri) 2185 (SC); AIR 2004 SC 3435: 2004 Cr LJ 2827:2004 AIR SCW 3051
Dilip Tiwari v State of Maharashtra, (2010) 1 SCC 77
Furman v Georgia 408 U.S. 238 (1972)
Kartar Singh v State Of Punjab 1994 SCC (3) 569, JT 1994 (2) 423
Kishore Singh Ravinder Dev v State of Rajasthan, AIR 1981 SC 625
Machhi Singh and Others v State of Punjab 1983 AIR 957, 1983 SCR (3) 413
Mahendra Nath Das v The Union of India and Others Writ Petition (Crl) No. 35/2011
Mithu v State of Punjab (1983) AIR 473, 1983 SCR (2) 690
Munuswamy v Unknown (1947) 1 MLJ 336
People v Anderson, 6 cal 3d 628, 649 (1971)

People's Union for Civil Liberties v State of Maharashtra & Anr. Unreported Order dated 30/3/2007 passed by the Bombay High Court in PIL No. 17/2007

Rajendra Prasad v State of Uttar Pradesh 1979 AIR 916, 1979 SCR (3) 78

Rajesh Kumar v State (2011) 13 SCC 706

Ravji @ Ram Chandra v State Of Rajasthan 1996 AIR 787, 1996 SCC (2) 175

Sant Gopal Alias Bhagat v State of U.P., 1995 CriLJ 312

Shatrughan Chauhan & Another v Union of India & Others, Writ Petition No. 55 of 2013, Supreme Court of India

Sher Singh and Others v State of Punjab AIR 1983 SC 465; 1983 SCR (2) 582, 591

Soering v United Kingdom, 161 Eur.Ct. H.R. (Ser.A) 34, (1989) 11 EHRR 439

State of Punjab v Devinder Pal Singh Bhullar & Ors. etc., AIR 2012 SC 364

Sunil Batra v Delhi Administration 1980 AIR 1579, 1980 SCR (2) 557

Triveniben v State of Gujrat, (1988) 4 AScc 574; (1989) 1 SCC, 678

Union Of India v Sriharan @, Murugan & Ors Writ Petition (Crl) No. 48 OF 2014, Supreme Court of India

Reports from Websites

Agency: IANS '*Tehelka founder and editor-in-chief Tarun Tejpal charged with rape, says he will aid probe*' DNA 22 November 2013. Available at: http://www.dnaindia.com/india/report-tehelka-founder-and-editor-in-chief-tarun-tejpal-charged-with-rape-says-he-will-aid-probe-1923326 (last accessed 17 March 2015).

Amnesty International India and People's Union for Civil Liberties (Tamil Nadu and Puducherry) '*Lethal Lottery: The Death Penalty in India – A study of Supreme Court judgments in death penalty cases 1950–2006*', 2008. Index number: ASA 20/007/2008. Available at: https://www.amnesty.org/en/documents/ASA20/007/2008/en/ (last accessed 25 March 2015).

Amnesty International Report '*Death sentences and executions 2011*' London. Index number: ACT 50/001/2012. Available at: https://www.amnesty.org/en/documents/ACT50/001/2012/en/ (last accessed 25 March 2015).

Areti, Krishna Kumari. '*Capital Punishment and Statutory Frame Work in India*'. Available at: http://works.bepress.com/krishnaareti/9 (2007). (last accessed 31 July 2015).

Fellner, Jamie and Mariner, Joanne. *Cold Storage: Super-maximum Security Confinement in Indiana*. Human Rights Watch, 1997. Available at: http://www.hrw.org/reports/1997/usind/ (last accessed 31 July 2015).

General Assembly Resolution 39/46, *Convention against Torture and Other Cruel, Inhuman or Degrading Treatment or Punishment* A/RES/39/46. Available at:

http://www.un.org/documents/ga/res/39/a39r046.htm (last accessed 25 March 2015).

General Assembly Resolution 44/128, *Elaboration of a second optional protocol to the International Civil and Political Rights, aiming at the abolition of the death penalty*, A/RES/44/128. Available at: http://www.un.org/documents/ga/res/44/a44r128.htm (last accessed 25 March 2015).

Harris, Lois Ruth and Gavin Thomas Lumsden Brown. 'Mixing interview and questionnaire methods: Practical problems in aligning data'. *Practical Assessment Research & Evaluation* 15, No. 1 (2010): 1–19. Available at http://pareonline.net/getvn.asp?v=15&n=1. (last accessed 31 July 2015).

Human Rights Council, *National report submitted in accordance with paragraph 5 of the annex to Human Rights Council resolution 16/21* – India, A/HRC/WG.6/13/IND/1, para. 28. Available at: http://daccess-dds-ny.un.org/doc/UNDOC/GEN/G12/116/85/PDF/G1211685.pdf?OpenElement (last accessed 25 March 2015).

Iyer, Krishna V.R. 'Capital punishment: A penological barbarity' *Mainstream* XLV, no. 45 (2007). Available at: http://www.mainstreamweekly.net/article394.html (last accessed 31 July 2015).

Jain, Neha and Sreekumar, R. *Behind Bars: A Closer Look at the Prison Visiting System*, The Commonwealth Human Rights Initiative, Madhya Pradesh, 2000. Available at: http://www.humanrightsinitiative.org/publications/prisons/prison_visiting_system.pdf (last accessed 31 July 2015).

Kearney, Helen. 'Children of Parents Sentenced to Death'. Quaker United Nations Office, 2012:145-166. Available at: http://www.quno.org/sites/default/files/resources/ENGLISH_Children%20of%20parents%20sentenced%20to%20death.pdf (last accessed 31 July 2015).

Maitra, Pradeep Kumar *After four years, 'Naxalite' Arun Ferreira walks free* Hindustan Times Nagpur, 4 January 2012. Available at: http://www.hindustantimes.com/india-news/after-four-years-naxalite-arun-ferreira-walks-free/article1-791172.aspx (last accessed 27 March 2015).

National Commission for the Protection of Human Subjects of Biomedical and Behavioural Research (NCPHSBBR) (1979) Belmont Report: Ethical Principles and Guidelines for the Protection of Human Subjects of Research, Department of Health, Education and Welfare, Office of the Secretary, Protection of Human Subjects. Available at: http://videocast.nih.gov/pdf/ohrp_appendix_belmont_report_vol_2.pdf (last accessed 10 November 2012).

National Crime Records Bureau. Prison Statistics India 2007. Available at: http://ncrb.nic.in/PSI-2011/Full/PSI-2011.pdf (last accessed 2 February 2013).

National Crime Records Bureau. Prison Statistics India 2013. Available at: http://ncrb.gov.in/ (last accessed 28 November 2014).

Nowak, Manfred. Foreword in Shalev, Sharon. *A sourcebook on solitary confinement.* London School of Economics and Political Science, London, (2008): n.p. Available at: http://solitaryconfinement.org/uploads/sourcebook_web.pdf (last accessed 31 July 2015).

Nowak, Manfred. *Torture and other cruel, inhuman or degrading treatment or punishment* A/63/175. Available at: http://daccess-dds-ny.un.org/doc/UNDOC/GEN/N08/440/75/PDF/N0844075.pdf?OpenElement (last accessed 25 March 2015).

Press Trust of India, '*Congress draft anti-rape law proposes chemical castration*', India Today 30 December 2012. Available at: http://indiatoday.intoday.in/story/congress-draft-anti-rape-law-proposes-chemical-castration/1/240107.html (last accessed 4 January 2015).

Roy, Arundhati. '*A perfect day for democracy*', The Hindu, 10 February 2013. Available at: http://www.thehindu.com/opinion/lead/a-perfect-day-for-democracy/article4397705.ece?homepage=true (last accessed 25 March 2015).

Sarang, Dastane and others. '*Ajmal Kasab loses composure at gallows, seeks forgiveness*' Times of India 22 November 2012. Available at: http://articles.timesofindia.indiatimes.com/2012-11-22/mumbai/35301740_1_ajmal-kasab-yerwada-jail-mumbai-s-arthur-road (last accessed 23 November 2013).

Sethi, Aman. '*Activists shocked at gallantry award for Chhattisgarh cop*'. The Hindu 14 February 2012. Available at: http://www.thehindu.com/news/national/article2834675.ece (last accessed 23 March 2015).

Shalev, Sharon. 'A sourcebook on solitary confinement'. London School of Economics and Political Science, London, 2008. Available at: http://solitaryconfinement.org/uploads/sourcebook_web.pdf (last accessed 31 July 2015).

Singh, Shiv Sahay. '*Park Street rape survivor Suzette Jordan dies*', The Hindu, 14 March 2015. Available at: http://www.thehindu.com/news/national/park-street-rape-victim-dies/article6989762.ece (last accessed 17 March 2015).

Utkarsh, Anand. 'SC admits PIL, will look into review of Presidential pardon'. The Indian Express 19 November 2013. Available at: http://archive.indianexpress.com/news/sc-admits-pil-will-look-into-review-of-presidential-pardon/1196646/ (last accessed 24 March 2015).

Vij, Shivam. '*Dalits, like flies to feudal lords*' Tehelka 4 November 2006. Available at: http://archive.tehelka.com/story_main22.asp?filename=Ne111106Dalits_like.asp (last accessed 23 March 2015).

World Development Report 2011, World Bank. Available at: http://siteresources.worldbank.org/INTWDRS/Resources/WDR2011_Full_Text.pdf (last accessed 24 March 2015).

Index